SNAKE TERMINOLOGY

SNAKE TERMINOLOGY

By

Manju Yadav

Lecturer
Department of Zoology
M.M.H. College
Ghaziabad (U.P.)
(India)

DISCOVERY PUBLISHING HOUSE PVT. LTD.
NEW DELHI-110 002

Published by:
Tilak Wasan

DISCOVERY PUBLISHING HOUSE PVT. LTD.
4383/4B, Ansari Road, Darya Ganj
New Delhi-110 002 (India)
Phone : +91-11-23279245, 43596064-65
Fax : +91-11-23253475
E-mail : discoverypublishinghouse@gmail.com
sales@discoverypublishinggroup.com
parul.wasan@gmail.com
web : www.discoverypublishinggroup.com

***First Edition:* 2013**

ISBN: 978-93-5056-304-5

Snake Terminology

Printed at:
Dynamic Printers
Delhi

Preface

Snakes are elongate, legless, carnivorous reptiles of the suborder Serpentes that can be distinguished from legless lizards by their lack of eyelids and external ears. Like all squamates, snakes are ectothermic, amniote vertebrates covered in overlapping scales. Many species of snakes have skulls with many more joints than their lizard ancestors, enabling them to swallow prey much larger than their heads with their highly mobile jaws. To accommodate their narrow bodies, snakes' paired organs (such as kidneys) appear one in front of the other instead of side by side, and most have only one functional lung. Some species retain a pelvic girdle with a pair of vestigial claws on either side of the cloaca.

Living snakes are found on most continents, except Antarctica and on many islands. Fifteen families are currently recognized, comprising 456 genera and over 2,900 species. They range in size from the tiny, 10 cm-long thread snake to pythons and anacondas of up to 7.6 metres (25 ft) in length. The recently discovered fossil *Titanoboa* was 15 metres (49 ft) long. Snakes are thought to have evolved from either burrowing or aquatic lizards during the Cretaceous period (*c* 150 Ma). The diversity of modern snakes appeared during the Paleocene period.

Modern snakes greatly diversified during the Paleocene. This occurred alongside the adaptive radiation of mammals, following the extinction of (non-avian) dinosaurs. The colubrids, one of the more common snake groups, became particularly diverse due to preying on rodents, an especially successful mammal group. There are over 2900 species of snakes ranging as far northward as the Arctic Circle in Scandinavia and southward through Australia and Tasmania. Snakes can be found on every continent (with the exception of Antarctica), in the sea, and as high as 16000 feet (4900 m) in the Himalayan Mountains of Asia. There are numerous islands from which snakes are absent, such as Ireland, Iceland, and New Zealand.

Cobras, vipers, and closely related species use venom to immobilize or kill their prey. The venom is modified saliva, delivered through fangs. The fangs of 'advanced' venomous snakes like viperids and elapids are hollow to inject venom more effectively, while the fangs of rear-fanged snakes such as the boomslang merely have a groove on the posterior edge to channel venom into the wound. Snake venoms are often prey specific, their role in self-defense is secondary.

Venom, like all salivary secretions, is a predigestant that initiates the breakdown of food into soluble compounds, facilitating proper digestion. Even non-venomous snake bites (like any animal bite) will cause tissue damage. It has recently been suggested that all snakes may be venomous to a certain degree, with harmless snakes having weak venom and no fangs. Most snakes currently labelled "nonvenomous" would still be considered harmless according to this theory, as they either lack a venom delivery method or are incapable of delivering enough to endanger a human. This theory postulates that snakes may have evolved from a common lizard ancestor that was venomous—and that venomous lizards like the gila monster, beaded lizard, monitor lizards, and the now-extinct mosasaurs may also have derived. They share this venom clade with various other saurian species.

Snakes do not ordinarily prey on humans, and most will not attack humans unless the snake is startled or injured, preferring instead to avoid contact. With the exception of large constrictors, nonvenomous snakes are not a threat to humans. The bite of nonvenomous snakes is usually harmless because their teeth are designed for grabbing and holding, rather than tearing or inflicting a deep puncture wound. Although the possibility of an infection and tissue damage is present in the bite of a nonvenomous snake, venomous snakes present far greater hazard to humans.

—Author

Contents

1 Introduction

Snakes are elongate, legless, carnivorous reptiles of the suborder Serpentes that can be distinguished from legless lizards by their lack of eyelids and external ears. Like all squamates, snakes are ectothermic, amniote vertebrates covered in overlapping scales. Many species of snakes have skulls with many more joints than their lizard ancestors, enabling them to swallow prey much larger than their heads with their highly mobile jaws. To accommodate their narrow bodies, snakes' paired organs (such as kidneys) appear one in front of the other instead of side by side, and most have only one functional lung. Some species retain a pelvic girdle with a pair of vestigial claws on either side of the cloaca.

Living snakes are found on most continents, except Antarctica and on many islands. Fifteen families are currently recognized, comprising 456 genera and over 2,900 species. They range in size from the tiny, 10 cm-long thread snake to pythons and anacondas of up to 7.6 metres (25 ft) in length. The recently discovered fossil *Titanoboa* was 15 metres (49 ft) long. Snakes are thought to have evolved from either burrowing or aquatic lizards during the Cretaceous period (*c* 150 Ma). The diversity of modern snakes appeared during the Paleocene period (*c* 66 to 56 Ma).

Most species are nonvenomous and those that have venom use it primarily to kill and subdue prey rather than for self-defense. Some possess venom potent enough to cause painful injury or death to humans. Non-venomous snakes either swallow prey alive or kill by constriction. The English word *snake* comes from Old English *snaca,* itself from Proto-Germanic *snak-an-* (cf. German *Schnake* 'ring snake', Swedish *snok* 'grass snake'), from Proto-Indo-European root *(s)neg-o-* 'to crawl, creep', which also gave *sneak* as well as Sanskrit *nagá* 'snake'. The word ousted *adder,* as *adder* went on to narrow in meaning, though in Old English *næddre* was the general word for snake. The other term, *serpent,* is from French, ultimately from Indo-European *serp-* (to creep), which also gave Greek *érpo* 'I crawl'.

The fossil record of snakes is relatively poor because snake skeletons are typically small and fragile, making fossilization uncommon. However, 150 million-year-old specimens, readily identifiable as snakes, yet with lizard-like skeletal structures, have been uncovered in South America and Africa. Based on comparative anatomy, there is consensus that snakes descended from lizards.

Pythons and boas—primitive groups among modern snakes—have vestigial hind limbs: tiny, clawed digits known as anal spurs, which are used to grasp during mating. The Leptotyphlopidae and Typhlopidae groups also possess remnants of the pelvic girdle, sometimes appearing as horny projections when visible.

Frontal limbs are nonexistent in all snakes. This is caused by the evolution of Hox genes, controlling limb morphogenesis. The axial skeleton of the snakes' common ancestor, like most other tetrapods, had regional specializations consisting of cervical (neck), thoracic (chest), lumbar (lower back), sacral (pelvic), and caudal (tail) vertebrae. Early in snake evolution, the Hox gene expression in the axial skeleton responsible for the development of the thorax became dominant. As a result, the vertebrae anterior to the hindlimb buds (when present) all have the same thoracic-like identity (except from the atlas, axis, and 1–3 neck vertebrae). In other words, most of a snake's skeleton is an extremely extended thorax. Ribs are found exclusively on the thoracic vertebrae. Neck, lumbar and pelvic vertebrae are very reduced in number (only 2-10 lumbar and pelvic vertebrae are present), while only a short tail remains of the caudal vertebrae. However, the tail is still long enough to be of important use in many species, and is modified in some aquatic and tree-dwelling species.

Modern snakes greatly diversified during the Paleocene. This occurred alongside the adaptive radiation of mammals, following the extinction of (non-avian) dinosaurs. The colubrids, one of the more common snake groups, became particularly diverse due to preying on rodents, an especially successful mammal group. There are over 2900 species of snakes ranging as far northward as the Arctic Circle in Scandinavia and southward through Australia and Tasmania. Snakes can be found on every continent (with the exception of Antarctica), in the sea, and as high as 16000 feet (4900 m) in the Himalayan Mountains of Asia. There are numerous islands from which snakes are absent, such as Ireland, Iceland, and New Zealand.

The origin of snakes remains an unresolved issue. There are two main hypotheses competing for acceptance.

Burrowing Lizard Hypothesis

There is fossil evidence to suggest that snakes may have evolved from burrowing lizards, such as the varanids (or a similar group) during the Cretaceous Period. An early fossil snake, *Najash rionegrina*, was a two-legged burrowing animal with a sacrum, and was fully terrestrial. One extant analog of these putative ancestors is the earless monitor *Lanthanotus* of Borneo (though it also is semiaquatic). Subterranean species evolved bodies streamlined for burrowing, and eventually lost their limbs. According to this hypothesis, features such as the transparent, fused eyelids (brille) and loss of external ears evolved to cope with fossorial difficulties, such as scratched corneas and dirt in the ears. Some primitive snakes are known to have possessed hindlimbs, but their pelvic bones lacked a direct connection to the vertebrae. These include fossil species like *Haasiophis, Pachyrhachis* and *Eupodophis,* which are slightly older than *Najash.*

Aquatic Mosasaur Hypothesis

An alternative hypothesis, based on morphology, suggests the ancestors of snakes were related to mosasaurs—extinct aquatic reptiles from the Cretaceous—which in turn are thought to have derived from varanid lizards. According to this hypothesis, the fused, transparent eyelids of snakes are thought to have evolved to combat marine conditions (corneal water loss through osmosis), and the external ears were lost through disuse in an aquatic environment. This ultimately lead to an animal similar to today's sea snakes. In the Late Cretaceous, snakes recolonized land, and continued to diversify into today's snakes. Fossilized snake remains are known from early Late Cretaceous marine sediments, which is consistent with this hypothesis; particularly so, as they are older than the terrestrial *Najash rionegrina*. Similar skull structure, reduced or absent limbs, and other anatomical features found in both mosasaurs and snakes lead to a positive cladistical correlation, although some of these features are shared with varanids.

Genetic studies in recent years have indicated snakes are not as closely related to monitor lizards as was once believed—and therefore not to mosasaurs, the proposed ancestor in the aquatic scenario of their evolution. However, more evidence links mosasaurs to snakes than to varanids. Fragmented remains found from the Jurassic and Early Cretaceous indicate deeper fossil records for these groups, which may potentially refute either hypothesis.

Taxonomy

All modern snakes are grouped within the suborder *Serpentes* in Linnean taxonomy, part of the order Squamata, though their precise placement within squamates is controversial.

There are two infraorders of *Serpentes*: Alethinophidia and Scolecophidia. This separation is based on morphological characteristics and mitochondrial DNA sequence similarity. Alethinophidia is sometimes split into Henophidia and Caenophidia, with the latter consisting of 'colubroid' snakes (colubrids, vipers, elapids, hydrophiids, and attractaspids) and acrochordids, while the other alethinophidian families comprise Henophidia. While not extant today, the Madtsoiidae, a family of giant, primitive, python-like snakes, was around until 50,000 years ago in Australia, represented by genera such as *Wonambi*.

There are numerous debates in the systematics within the group. For instance, many sources classify Boidae and Pythonidae as one family, while some keep the Elapidae and Hydrophiidae separate for practical reasons despite their extremely close relation.

The molecular studies support the monophyly of the clades of modern snakes, scolecophidians, typhlopids + anomalepidids, alethinophidians, core alethinophidians, uropeltids (*Cylindrophis, Anomochilus,* uropeltines), macrostomatans, booids, boids, pythonids and caenophidians.

Skeleton

The skeleton of most snakes consists solely of the skull, hyoid, vertebral column, and ribs, though henophidian snakes retain vestiges of the pelvis and rear limbs. The skull of the snake consists of a solid and complete braincase, to which many of the other bones are only loosely attached, particularly the highly mobile jaw bones, which facilitate manipulation and ingestion of large prey items. The left and right sides of the lower jaw are joined only by a flexible ligament at the anterior tips, allowing them to separate widely, while the posterior end of the lower jaw bones articulate with a quadrate bone, allowing further mobility. The bones of the mandible and quadrate bones can also pick up ground borne vibrations. The hyoid is a small bone located posterior and ventral to the skull, in the 'neck' region, which serves as an attachment for muscles of the snake's tongue, as it does in all other tetrapods.

The vertebral column consists of anywhere between 200 to 400 (or more) vertebrae. Tail vertebrae are comparatively few in number (often less than 20% of the total) and lack ribs, while body vertebrae each have two ribs articulating with them. The vertebrae have projections that allow for strong muscle attachment enabling locomotion without limbs. Autotomy of the tail, a feature found in some lizards is absent in most snakes. Caudal autotomy in snakes is rare and is intervertebral, unlike that in lizards, which is intravertebral—that is, the break happens along a predefined fracture plane present on a vertebra.

In some snakes, most notably boas and pythons, there are vestiges of the hindlimbs in the form of a pair of pelvic spurs. These small, claw-like protrusions on each side of the cloaca are the external portion of the vestigial hindlimb skeleton, which includes the remains of an ilium and femur.

Internal Organs

The snake's heart is encased in a sac, called the *pericardium*, located at the bifurcation of the bronchi. The heart is able to move around, however, owing to the lack of a diaphragm. This adjustment protects the heart from potential damage when large ingested prey is passed through the esophagus. The spleen is attached to the gall bladder and pancreas and filters the blood. The thymus gland is located in fatty tissue above the heart and is responsible for the generation of immune cells in the blood. The cardiovascular system of snakes is also unique for the presence of a renal portal system in which the blood from the snake's tail passes through the kidneys before returning to the heart.

The vestigial left lung is often small or sometimes even absent, as snakes' tubular bodies require all of their organs to be long and thin. In the majority of species, only one lung is functional. This lung contains a vascularized anterior portion and a posterior portion that does not function in gas exchange. This 'saccular lung' is used for hydrostatic purposes to adjust buoyancy in some aquatic snakes and its function remains unknown in terrestrial species. Many organs that are paired, such as kidneys or reproductive organs, are staggered within the body, with one located ahead of the other.

Size

The now extinct *Titanoboa cerrejonensis* snakes found were 12-15 meters (39-49 ft) in length. By comparison, the largest extant snakes are the reticulated python, which measures about 9 meters (30 ft) long, and the anaconda, which measures about 7.5 meters (25 ft) long and is considered the heaviest snake on Earth.

At the other end of the scale, the smallest extant snake is *Leptotyphlops carlae*, with a length of about 10 centimeters (4 in). Most snakes are fairly small animals, approximately 3 feet in length.

Skin

The skin of a snake is covered in scales. Contrary to the popular notion of snakes being slimy because of possible confusion of snakes with worms, snakeskin has a smooth, dry texture. Most snakes use specialized belly scales to travel, gripping surfaces. The body scales may be smooth, keeled, or granular. The eyelids of a snake are transparent "spectacle" scales, which remain permanently closed, also known as brille.

The shedding of scales is called *ecdysis* (or in normal usage, *moulting* or *sloughing*). In the case of snakes, the complete outer layer of skin is shed in one layer. Snake scales are not discrete, but extensions of the epidermis—hence they are not shed separately but as a complete outer layer during each moult, akin to a sock being turned inside out.

The shape and number of scales on the head, back, and belly are often characteristic and used for taxonomic purposes. Scales are named mainly according to their positions on the body. In 'advanced' (Caenophidian) snakes, the broad belly scales and rows of dorsal scales correspond to the vertebrae, allowing scientists to count the vertebrae without dissection.

Snakes' eyes are covered by their clear scales (the brille) rather than movable eyelids. Their eyes are always open, and for sleeping, the retina can be closed or the face buried among the folds of the body.

Moulting serves a number of functions. Firstly, the old and worn skin is replaced; secondly, it helps get rid of parasites such as mites and ticks. Renewal of the skin by moulting is supposed to allow growth in some animals such as insects; however, this has been disputed in the case of snakes.

Moulting occurs periodically throughout a snake's life. Before a moult, the snake stops eating and often hides or moves to a safe place. Just before shedding, the skin becomes dull and dry looking and the eyes become cloudy or blue-coloured. The inner surface of the old skin liquefies. This causes the old skin to separate from the new skin beneath it. After a few days, the eyes clear and the snake "crawls" out of its old skin. The old skin breaks near the mouth and the snake wriggles out, aided by rubbing against rough surfaces. In many cases, the cast skin peels backward over the body from head to tail in one piece, like pulling a sock off inside-out. A new, larger, brighter layer of skin has formed underneath.

An older snake may shed its skin only once or twice a year. But a younger snake, still growing, may shed up to four times a year. The discarded skin gives a perfect imprint of the scale pattern, and it is usually possible to identify the snake if the discarded skin is reasonably intact. This periodic renewal has led to the snake being a symbol of healing and medicine, as pictured in the Rod of Asclepius.

Eyesight

Snake vision varies greatly, from only being able to distinguish light from dark to keen eyesight, but the main trend is that their vision is adequate although not sharp, and allows them to track movements. Generally, vision is best in arboreal snakes and weakest in burrowing snakes. Some snakes, such as the Asian vine snake (genus *Ahaetulla*), have binocular vision, with both eyes capable of focusing on the same point. Most snakes focus by moving the lens back and forth in relation to the retina, while in the other amniote groups, the lens is stretched.

Smell

Snakes use smell to track their prey. They smell by using their forked tongues to collect airborne particles, then passing them to the vomeronasal organ or *Jacobson's organ* in the mouth for examination. The fork in the tongue gives snakes a sort of directional sense of smell and taste simultaneously. They keep their tongues constantly in motion, sampling particles from the air, ground, and water, analyzing the chemicals found, and determining the presence of prey or predators in the local environment. In water-dwelling snakes, such as the Anaconda, the tongue functions efficiently under water.

The part of the body in direct contact with the ground is very sensitive to vibration; thus, a snake can sense other animals approaching by detecting faint vibrations in the air and on the ground.

Infrared Sensitivity

Pit vipers, pythons, and some boas have infrared-sensitive receptors in deep grooves between the nostril and eye, although some have labial pits on their upper lip just below the nostrils (common in pythons), which allow them to "see" the radiated heat of warm-blooded prey mammals.

Venom

Milk snakes are often mistaken for coral snakes, whose venom is deadly to humans.

Cobras, vipers, and closely related species use venom to immobilize or kill their prey. The venom is modified saliva, delivered through fangs. The fangs of 'advanced' venomous snakes like viperids and elapids are hollow to inject venom more effectively, while the fangs of rear-fanged snakes such as the boomslang merely have a groove on the posterior edge to channel venom into the wound. Snake venoms are often prey specific, their role in self-defense is secondary.

Venom, like all salivary secretions, is a predigestant that initiates the breakdown of food into soluble compounds, facilitating proper digestion. Even nonvenomous snake bites (like any animal bite) will cause tissue damage.

Certain birds, mammals, and other snakes (such as kingsnakes) that prey on venomous snakes have developed resistance and even immunity to certain venoms. Venomous snakes include three families of snakes, and do not constitute a formal classification group used in taxonomy.

The term poisonous snake is mostly incorrect. Poison is inhaled or ingested, whereas venom is injected. There are, however, two exceptions: *Rhabdophis* sequesters toxins from the toads it eats, then secretes them from nuchal glands to ward off predators, and a small population of garter snakes in Oregon retains enough toxin in their liver from the newts they eat to be effectively poisonous to small local predators (such as crows and foxes).

Snake venoms are complex mixtures of proteins, and are stored in poison glands at the back of the head. In all venomous snakes, these glands open through ducts into grooved or hollow teeth in the upper jaw. These proteins can potentially be a mix of neurotoxins (which attack the nervous system), hemotoxins (which attack the circulatory system), cytotoxins, bungarotoxins and many other toxins that affect the body in different ways. Almost all snake venom contains *hyaluronidase*, an enzyme that ensures rapid diffusion of the venom.

Venomous snakes that use hemotoxins usually have fangs in the front of their mouths, making it easier for them to inject the venom into their victims. Some snakes that use neurotoxins (such as the mangrove snake) have fangs in the back of their mouths, with the fangs curled backwards. This makes it both difficult for the snake to use its venom and for scientists to milk them. *Elapids*, however, such as cobras and kraits are *proteroglyphous*—they possess hollow fangs that cannot be erected toward the front of their mouths, and cannot "stab" like a viper. They must actually bite the victim.

It has recently been suggested that all snakes may be venomous to a certain degree, with harmless snakes having weak venom and no fangs. Most snakes currently labelled "nonvenomous" would still be considered harmless according to this theory, as they either lack a venom delivery method or are incapable of delivering enough to endanger a human. This theory postulates that snakes may have evolved from a common lizard ancestor that was venomous—and that venomous lizards like the gila monster, beaded lizard, monitor lizards, and the now-extinct mosasaurs may also have derived. They share this venom clade with various other saurian species.

Venomous snakes are classified in two taxonomic families:

1. *Elapids* – cobras including king cobras, kraits, mambas, Australian copperheads, sea snakes, and coral snakes.
2. *Viperids* – vipers, rattlesnakes, copperheads/cottonmouths, adders and bushmasters.

There is a third family containing the *opistoglyphous* (rear-fanged) snakes (as well as the majority of other snake species):

Colubrids – boomslangs, tree snakes, vine snakes, mangrove snakes, although not all colubrids are venomous.

Feeding and Diet

All snakes are strictly carnivorous, eating small animals including lizards, other snakes, small mammals, birds, eggs, fish, snails or insects. Because snakes cannot bite or tear their food to pieces, they must swallow prey whole. The body size of a snake has a major influence on its eating habits. Smaller snakes eat smaller prey. Juvenile pythons might start out feeding on lizards or mice and graduate to small deer or antelope as an adult, for example.

The snake's jaw is a complex structure. Contrary to the popular belief that snakes can dislocate their jaws, snakes have a very flexible lower jaw, the two halves of which are not rigidly attached, and numerous other joints in their skull, allowing them to open their mouths wide enough to swallow their prey whole, even if it is larger in diameter than the snake itself, as snakes do not chew. For example, the African egg-eating snake has flexible jaws adapted for eating eggs much larger than the diameter of its head. This snake has no teeth, but does have bony protrusions on the inside edge of its spine, which it uses to break shells when it eats eggs.

While the majority of snakes eat a variety of prey animals, there is some specialization by some species. King cobras and the Australian bandy-bandy consume other snakes. *Pareas iwesakii* and other snail-eating colubrids of subfamily Pareatinae have more teeth on the right side of their mouths than on the left, as the shells of their prey usually spiral clockwise.

Some snakes have a venomous bite, which they use to kill their prey before eating it. Other snakes kill their prey by constriction. Still others swallow their prey whole and alive.

After eating, snakes become dormant while the process of digestion takes place. Digestion is an intense activity, especially after consumption of large prey. In species that feed only sporadically, the entire intestine enters a reduced state between meals to conserve energy. The digestive system is then 'up-regulated' to full capacity within 48 hours of prey consumption. Being ectothermic ("cold-blooded"), the surrounding temperature plays a large role in snake digestion. The ideal temperature for snakes to digest is 30ºC (86ºF). So much metabolic energy is involved in a snake's digestion that in the Mexican rattlesnake (*Crotalus durissus*), surface body temperature increases by as much as 1.2ºC (2.2ºF) during the digestive process. Because of this, a snake disturbed after having eaten recently will often regurgitate its prey to be able to escape the perceived threat. When undisturbed, the digestive process is highly efficient, with the snake's digestive enzymes dissolving and absorbing everything but the prey's hair (or feathers) and claws, which are excreted along with waste.

Locomotion

The lack of limbs does not impede the movement of snakes. They have developed several different modes of locomotion to deal with particular environments. Unlike the gaits of limbed animals, which form a continuum, each mode of snake locomotion is discrete and distinct from the others; transitions between modes are abrupt.

Lateral Undulation

Lateral undulation is the sole mode of aquatic locomotion, and the most common mode of terrestrial locomotion. In this mode, the body of the snake alternately flexes to the left and right, resulting in a series of rearward-moving 'waves'. While this movement appears rapid, snakes have rarely been documented moving faster than two body-lengths per second, often much less. This mode of movement has the same net cost of transport (calories burned per meter moved) as running in lizards of the same mass.

Terrestrial

Terrestrial lateral undulation is the most common mode of terrestrial locomotion for most snake species. In this mode, the posteriorly moving waves push against contact points in the environment, such as rocks, twigs, irregularities in the soil, etc. Each of these environmental objects, in turn, generates a reaction force directed forward and towards the midline of the snake, resulting in forward thrust while the lateral components cancel out. The speed of this movement depends upon the density of push-points in the environment, with a medium density of about 8 along the snake's length being ideal. The wave speed is precisely the same as the snake speed, and as a result, every point on the snake's body follows the path of the point ahead of it, allowing snakes to move through very dense vegetation and small openings.

Aquatic

When swimming, the waves become larger as they move down the snake's body, and the wave travels backwards faster than the snake moves forwards. Thrust is generated by pushing their body against the water, resulting in the observed slip. In spite of overall similarities, studies show that the pattern of muscle activation is different in aquatic versus terrestrial lateral undulation, which justifies calling them separate modes. All snakes can laterally undulate forward (with backward-moving waves), but only sea snakes have been observed reversing the motion (moving backwards with forward-moving waves).

Sidewinding

Most often employed by colubroid snakes (colubrids, elapids, and vipers) when the snake must move in an environment that lacks irregularities to push against (rendering lateral undulation impossible), such as a slick mud flat, or a sand dune. Sidewinding is a modified form of lateral undulation in which all of the body segments oriented in one direction remain in contact with the ground, while the other segments are lifted up, resulting in a peculiar "rolling" motion. This mode of locomotion overcomes the slippery nature of sand or mud by pushing off with only static portions on the body, thereby minimizing slipping. The static nature of the contact points can be shown from the tracks of a sidewinding snake, which show each belly scale imprint, without any smearing. This mode of locomotion has very low caloric cost, less than ? of the cost for a lizard or snake to move the same distance. Contrary to popular belief, there is no evidence that sidewinding is associated with the sand being hot.

Concertina

When push-points are absent, but there is not enough space to use sidewinding because of lateral constraints, such as in tunnels, snakes rely on concertina locomotion. In this mode, the snake braces the posterior portion of its body against the tunnel wall while the front of the snake extends and straightens. The front portion then flexes and forms an anchor point, and the posterior is straightened and pulled forwards. This mode of locomotion is slow and very demanding, up to seven times the cost of laterally undulating over the same distance. This high cost is due to the repeated stops and starts of portions of the body as well as the necessity of using active muscular effort to brace against the tunnel walls.

Rectilinear

The slowest mode of snake locomotion is rectilinear locomotion, which is also the only one where the snake does not need to bend its body laterally, though it may do so when turning. In this mode, the belly scales are lifted and pulled forward before being placed down and the body pulled over them. Waves of movement and stasis pass posteriorly, resulting in a series of ripples in the skin. The ribs of the snake do not move in this mode of locomotion and this method is most often used by large pythons, boas, and vipers when stalking prey across open ground as the snake's movements are subtle and harder to detect by their prey in this manner.

Other

The movement of snakes in arboreal habitats has only recently been studied. While on tree branches, snakes use several modes of locomotion depending on species and bark texture. In general, snakes will use a modified form of concertina locomotion on smooth branches, but will laterally undulate if contact points are available. Snakes move faster on small branches and when contact points are present, in contrast to limbed animals, which do better on large branches with little 'clutter'.

Gliding snakes (*Chrysopelea*) of Southeast Asia launch themselves from branch tips, spreading their ribs and laterally undulating as they glide between trees. These snakes can perform a controlled glide for hundreds of feet depending upon launch altitude and can even turn in midair.

Reproduction

Although a wide range of reproductive modes are used by snakes, all snakes employ internal fertilization. This is accomplished by means of paired, forked hemipenes, which are stored, inverted, in the male's tail. The hemipenes are often grooved, hooked, or spined in order to grip the walls of the female's cloaca.

Most species of snakes lay eggs, but most snakes abandon the eggs shortly after laying. However, a few species (such as the King cobra) actually construct nests and stay in the vicinity of the hatchlings after incubation. Most pythons coil around their egg-clutches and remain with them until they hatch. A female python will not leave the eggs, except to occasionally bask in the sun or drink water. She will even 'shiver' to generate heat to incubate the eggs.

Some species of snake are ovoviviparous and retain the eggs within their bodies until they are almost ready to hatch. Recently, it has been confirmed that several species of snake are fully viviparous, such as the boa constrictor and green anaconda, nourishing their young through a placenta as well as a yolk sac, which is highly unusual among reptiles, or anything else outside of placental mammals. Retention of eggs and live birth are most often associated with colder environments, as the retention of the young within the female.

Snakes do not ordinarily prey on humans, and most will not attack humans unless the snake is startled or injured, preferring instead to avoid contact. With the exception of large constrictors, nonvenomous snakes are not a threat to humans. The bite of nonvenomous snakes is usually harmless because their teeth are designed for grabbing and holding, rather than tearing or inflicting a deep puncture wound. Although the possibility of an infection and tissue damage is present in the bite of a nonvenomous snake, venomous snakes present far greater hazard to humans.

Documented deaths resulting from snake bites are uncommon. Nonfatal bites from venomous snakes may result in the need for amputation of a limb or part thereof. Of the roughly 725 species of venomous snakes worldwide, only 250 are able to kill a human with one bite. Australia averages only one fatal snake bite per year. In India, 250,000 snakebites are recorded in a single year, with as many as 50,000 recorded initial deaths.

The treatment for a snakebite is as variable as the bite itself. The most common and effective method is through antivenom (or antivenin), a serum made from the venom of the snake. Some antivenom is species specific (monovalent) while some is made for use with multiple species in mind (polyvalent). In the United States for example, all species of venomous snakes are pit vipers, with the exception of the coral snake. To produce antivenom, a mixture of the venoms of the different species of rattlesnakes, copperheads, and cottonmouths is injected into the body of a horse in ever-increasing dosages until the horse is immunized. Blood is then extracted from the immunized horse; the serum is separated and further purified and freeze-dried. It is reconstituted with sterile water and becomes antivenom. For this reason, people who are allergic to horses are more likely to suffer an allergic reaction to antivenom. Antivenom for the more dangerous species (such as mambas, taipans, and cobras) is made in a similar manner in India, South Africa, and Australia, although these antivenoms are species-specific.

In some parts of the world, especially in India, snake charming is a roadside show performed by a charmer. In such a show, the snake charmer carries a basket that contains a snake that he seemingly charms by playing tunes from his flutelike musical instrument, to which the snake responds. Snakes lack external ears, though they do have internal ears, and respond to the movement of the flute, not the actual noise.

The Wildlife Protection Act of 1972 in India technically proscribes snake charming on grounds of reducing animal cruelty. Other snake charmers also have a snake and mongoose show, where both the animals have a mock fight; however, this is not very common, as the snakes, as well as the mongooses, may be seriously injured or killed. Snake charming as a profession is dying out in India because of competition from modern forms of entertainment and environment laws proscribing the practice.

Trapping

The *Irulas* tribe of Andhra Pradesh and Tamil Nadu in India have been hunter-gatherers in the hot, dry plains forests, and have practised the art of snake catching for generations. They have a vast knowledge of snakes in the field. They generally catch the snakes with the help of a simple stick. Earlier, the *Irulas* caught thousands of snakes for the snake-skin industry. After the complete ban on snake-skin industry in India and protection of all snakes under the Indian Wildlife (Protection) Act 1972, they formed the Irula Snake Catcher's Cooperative and switched to catching snakes for removal of venom, releasing them in the wild after four extractions. The venom so collected is used for producing life-saving antivenom, biomedical research and for other medicinal products. The *Irulas* are also known to eat some of the snakes they catch and are very useful in rat extermination in the villages.

Despite the existence of snake charmers, there have also been professional snake catchers or wranglers. Modern-day snake trapping involves a herpetologist using a long stick with a V-shaped end. Some television show hosts, like Bill Haast, Austin Stevens, Steve Irwin, and Jeff Corwin, prefer to catch them using bare hands.

While not commonly thought of as food in most cultures, in some cultures, the consumption of snakes is acceptable, or even considered a delicacy, prized for its alleged pharmaceutical effect of warming the heart. Snake soup of Cantonese cuisine is consumed by local people in autumn, to warm up their body. Western cultures document the consumption of snakes under extreme circumstances of hunger. Cooked rattlesnake meat is an exception, which is commonly consumed in parts of the Midwestern United States. In Asian countries such as China, Taiwan, Thailand, Indonesia, Vietnam and Cambodia, drinking the blood of snakes—particularly the cobra—is believed to increase sexual virility. The blood is drained while the cobra is still alive when possible, and is usually mixed with some form of liquor to improve the taste.

In some Asian countries, the use of snakes in alcohol is also accepted. In such cases, the body of a snake or several snakes is left to steep in a jar or container of liquor. It is claimed that this makes the liquor stronger (as well as more expensive). One example of this is the Habu snake sometimes placed in the Okinawan liquor Awamori also known as 'Habu Sake'.

U.S. Army Special Forces trainees are taught to catch, kill, and eat snakes during their survival course; this has earned them the nickname 'snake eaters', which the video game Metal Gear Solid 3: Snake Eater may be inferred to draw from.

Snake wine is an alcoholic beverage produced by infusing whole snakes in rice wine or grain alcohol. The drink was first recorded to have been consumed in China during the Western Zhou dynasty and considered an important curative and believed to reinvigorate a person according to Traditional Chinese medicine.

In the Western world, some snakes (especially docile species such as the ball python and corn snake) are kept as pets. To meet this demand a captive breeding industry has developed. Snakes bred in captivity tend to make better pets and are considered preferable to wild caught specimens. Snakes can be very low maintenance pets, especially compared to more traditional species. They require minimal space, as most common species do not exceed five feet in length. Pet snakes can be fed relatively infrequently, usually once every 5-14 days. Certain snakes have a lifespan of more than 40 years if given proper care.

Symbolism

In Egyptian history, the snake occupies a primary role with the Nile cobra adorning the crown of the pharaoh in ancient times. It was worshipped as one of the gods and was also used for sinister purposes: murder of an adversary and ritual suicide (Cleopatra).

In Greek mythology snakes are often associated with deadly and dangerous antagonists, but this is not to say that snakes are symbolic of evil; in fact, snakes are a chthonic symbol, roughly translated as 'earthbound'. The nine-headed Lernaean Hydra that Hercules defeated and the three Gorgon sisters are children of Gaia, the earth. Medusa was one of the three Gorgon sisters who Perseus defeated. Medusa is described as a hideous mortal, with snakes instead of hair and the power to turn men to stone with her gaze. After killing her, Perseus gave her head to Athena who fixed it to her shield called the Aegis. The Titans are also depicted in art with snakes instead of legs and feet for the same reason—they are children of Gaia and Ouranos (Uranus), so they are bound to the earth.

Three medical symbols involving snakes that are still used today are Bowl of Hygieia, symbolizing pharmacy, and the Caduceus and Rod of Asclepius, which are symbols denoting medicine in general.

India is often called the land of snakes and is steeped in tradition regarding snakes. Snakes are worshipped as gods even today with many women pouring milk on snake pits (despite snakes' aversion for milk). The cobra is seen on the neck of Shiva and Vishnu is depicted often as sleeping on a seven-headed snake or within the coils of a serpent. There are also several temples in India solely for cobras sometimes called *Nagraj* (King of Snakes) and it is believed that snakes are symbols of fertility. There is a Hindu festival called Nag Panchami each year on which day snakes are venerated and prayed to.

In India there is another mythology about snakes. Commonly known in Hindi as *'ichchhadhari'* snakes. Such snakes can take the form of any living creature, but prefer human form. These mythical snakes possess a valuable gem called *'mani'*, which is more brilliant than diamond. There are many stories in India about greedy people trying to possess this gem and ending up getting killed.

The Ouroboros is a symbol associated with many different religions and customs, and is claimed to be related to Alchemy. The Ouroboros or Oroboros is a snake eating its own tail in a clock-wise direction (from the head to the tail) in the shape of a circle, representing manifestation of one's own life and rebirth, leading to immortality.

The snake is one of the 12 celestial animals of Chinese Zodiac, in the Chinese calendar.

Many ancient Peruvian cultures worshipped nature. They emphasized animals and often depicted snakes in their art.

Snakes are a part of Hindu worship. A festival *Nag Panchami* is celebrated every year on snakes. Most images of Lord Shiva depict snake around his neck. *Puranas* have various stories associated with Snakes. In the *Puranas*, Shesha is said to hold all the planets of the Universe on his hoods and to constantly sing the glories of Vishnu from all his mouths. He is sometimes referred to as *'Ananta-Shesha'*, which means *'Endless Shesha'*. Other notable snakes in Hinduism are Ananta, Vasuki, Taxak, Karkotaka and Pingala. The term Naga is used to refer to entities that take the form of large snakes in Hinduism and Buddhism.

Snakes have also been widely revered, such as in ancient Greece, where the serpent was seen as a healer, and Asclepius carried two intertwined on his wand, a symbol seen today on many ambulances.

In religious terms, the snake is arguably the most important animal in ancient Mesoamerica. "In states of ecstasy, lords dance a serpent dance; great descending snakes adorn and support buildings from Chichen Itza to Tenochtitlan, and the Nahuatl word *coatl* meaning serpent or twin, forms part of primary deities such as Mixcoatl, Quetzalcoatl, and Coatlicue." In both Maya and Aztec calendars, the fifth day of the week was known as Snake Day.

In Judaism, the snake of brass is also a symbol of healing, of one's life being saved from imminent death.

In Christianity, Christ's redemptive work is compared to saving one's life through beholding the Nehushtan (serpent of brass). Snake handlers use snakes as an integral part of church worship in order to exhibit their faith in divine protection. However, more commonly in Christianity, the serpent has been seen as a representative of evil and sly plotting, which can be seen in the description in Genesis chapter 3 of a snake in the Garden of Eden tempting Eve. Saint Patrick is reputed to have expelled all snakes from Ireland while Christianising the country in the 5th century, thus explaining the absence of snakes there.

In Christianity and Judaism, the snake makes its infamous appearance in the first book of the *Bible* when a serpent appears before the first couple Adam and Eve and tempts them with the forbidden fruit from the Tree of Knowledge. The snake returns in Exodus when Moses, as a sign of God's power, turns his staff into a snake and when Moses made the

Nehushtan, a bronze snake on a pole that when looked at cured the people of bites from the snakes that plagued them in the desert. The serpent makes its final appearance symbolizing Satan in the Book of Revelation: "And he laid hold on the dragon the old serpent, which is the devil and Satan, and bound him for a thousand years."

In Neo-Paganism and Wicca, the snake is seen as a symbol of wisdom and knowledge.

2 Venomous Elapid Snakes

Sea snakes are venomous elapid snakes that inhabit marine environments for most or all of their lives. Though they evolved from terrestrial ancestors, most are extensively adapted to a fully aquatic life and are unable to even move on land, except for the genus *Laticauda*, which retain ancestral characteristics which allow limited land movement. They are found in warm coastal waters from the Indian Ocean to the Pacific. All have paddle-like tails and many have laterally compressed bodies that give them an eel-like appearance. Unlike fish, they do not have gills and must surface regularly to breathe. They are among the most completely aquatic of all air-breathing vertebrates. Among this group are species with some of the most potent venoms of all snakes. Some have gentle dispositions and bite only when provoked, but others are much more aggressive. Currently, 17 genera are described as sea snakes, comprising 62 species.

Adults of most species grow to between 120-150 cm (3.9-4.9 ft) in length, with the largest, *Hydrophis spiralis*, reaching a maximum of 3 m (9.8 ft). Their eyes are relatively small with a round pupil and most have nostrils that are located dorsally. The skulls do not differ significantly from terrestrial elapids, although the dentition is relatively primitive with short fangs and (with the exception of *Emydocephalus*) as many as 18 smaller teeth behind them on the maxilla.

Most sea snakes are completely aquatic and have adapted to their environment in many ways, the most characteristic of which is a paddle-like tail that has increased their swimming ability. To a varying degree, the bodies of many species are laterally compressed, especially in the pelagic species. This has often caused the ventral scales to become reduced in size, even difficult to distinguish from the adjoining scales. Their lack of ventral scales means that they have become virtually helpless on land, but as they live out their entire life cycle at sea, they have no need to leave the water.

The only genus that has retained the enlarged ventral scales is the sea kraits, *Laticauda*, with only five species. These snakes are considered to be more primitive, as they still spend much of their time on land, where their ventral scales afford them the necessary grip. *Laticauda* are also the only sea snakes with internasal scales, i.e., their nostrils are not located dorsally.

As it is easier for a snake's tongue to fulfil its olfactory function under water, its action is short compared to that of terrestrial snake species. Only the forked tips protrude from the mouth through a divided notch in the middle of the rostral scale. The nostrils have valves consisting of a specialized spongy tissue to exclude water, and the windpipe can be drawn up to where the short nasal passage opens into the roof of the mouth. This an important adaptation for an animal that must surface to breathe, but may have its head partially submerged when doing so. The lung has become very large and extends almost the entire length of the body, although it is thought that the rear portion developed to aid buoyancy rather than to exchange gas. It is also possible that the extended lung serves to store air for dives.

Most sea snakes are able to respire through their skin. This is unusual for reptiles, because their skin is thick and scaly, but experiments with the black-and-yellow sea snake, *Pelamis platurus* (a pelagic species), have shown that this species can satisfy about 20 per cent of its oxygen requirements in this manner, which allows for prolonged dives.

Like other land animals that have adapted to life in a marine environment, sea snakes ingest considerably more salt than their terrestrial relatives through their diet and when sea water is inadvertently swallowed.

This meant that they had to evolve a more effective means of regulating the salt concentration of their blood. Mammals have the advantage of being able to pass salt in solution, mostly in the urine, but kidney function in birds and reptiles is too weak to remove salt in sufficient amounts. In birds, such as penguins, salt is removed through nasal glands, just as with the marine iguanas of the Galapagos Islands. Sea turtles have lacrimal glands that allow them to produce very salty tears. In sea snakes, the posterior sublingual glands, located under and around the tongue sheath, evolved to allow them to expel salt with their tongue action.

Scalation among sea snakes is highly variable. As opposed to terrestrial snake species that have imbricate scales to protect against abrasion, the scales of most pelagic sea snakes do not overlap. Reef dwelling species, such as *Aypisurus*, do have imbricate scales to protect against the sharp coral. The scales themselves may be smooth, keeled, spiny or granular, the latter often looking like warts. *Pelamis* has body scales that are 'peg-like', while those on its tail are juxtaposed hexagonal plates.

Aipysurus laevis has been found to have photoreceptors in the skin of its tail, allowing it to detect light and presumably aiding it to remain hidden inside coral holes during the day. While other species have not been tested, it is possible that *A. laevis* is not unique among sea snakes in this respect.

Sea snakes are mostly confined to the warm tropical waters of the Indian Ocean and the western Pacific Ocean, with a few species found well out into Oceania. The geographic range of one species, *Pelamis platurus*, is wider than that of any other reptile species, save for a few species of sea turtles. It extends from the east coast of Africa, from Djibouti in the north to Cape Town in the south, across the Indian Ocean, the Pacific, south as far as the northern coast of New Zealand, all the way to the western coast of the Americas, where it occurs from northern Peru in the south (including the Galápagos Islands) to the Gulf of California in the north. Isolated specimens have been found as far north as San Clemente in the United States.

Sea snakes do not occur in the Atlantic Ocean. It is thought that *Pelamis* would be found there were it not for the cold currents off Namibia and western South Africa that keep it from crossing into the eastern South Atlantic, or south of 5° latitude along the South American west coast. Sea snakes do not occur in the Red Sea, believed to be due to its increased salinity, so there is no danger of them crossing through the Suez Canal. Salinity, or rather a lack thereof, is also thought to be the reason why *Pelamis* has not crossed into the Caribbean via the Panama Canal.

Despite their marine adaptations, most sea snakes prefer shallow waters near land, around islands, and especially waters that are somewhat sheltered, as well as near estuaries. They may swim up rivers and have been reported as far as 160 km (99 mi) from the sea. Others, such as *Pelamis platurus*, are pelagic and are found in drift lines; slicks of floating debris brought together by surface currents. Some sea snakes inhabit mangrove swamps and similar brackish water habitats and there are two landlocked fresh water forms: *Hydrophis semperi* occurs in Lake Taal in the Philippines, and *Laticauda crockeri* in Lake Te Nggano on Rennell Island in the Solomon Islands.

Behaviour

Stidworthy describes all sea snake species as being reluctant to bite, and Fichter adds that they are quite docile. Researchers also claims they are mainly non-aggressive. The US Navy describes sea snakes as generally mild tempered, although there is variation among species and individuals. Researcher suggests that species such as *Pelamis platurus*, that feed by simply gulping down their prey, are more likely to bite when provoked because they seem to use their venom more for defence. This is in contrast to others, such as *Laticauda*, that use their venom for prey immobilization; these snakes are frequently handled with impunity by local fishermen. Species that have been reported as much more aggressive include *Aipysurus laevis, Astrotia stokesii, Enhydrina schistosa* and *Hydrophis ornatus*.

Researcher mentions that when they are taken out of the water, their movements become very erratic. They crawl awkwardly in these situations and can become quite aggressive, striking wildly at anything that moves. Yet they are frequently caught in nets by fishermen, who unravel and throw them back into the water barehanded, usually suffering no harm. On land, sea snakes are unable to coil and strike like terrestrial snakes.

Observations suggest that sea snakes are active both day and night. In the morning, and sometimes late in the afternoon, they can be seen at the surface basking in the sunlight. When disturbed, they dive below. Sea snakes have been reported swimming at depths of over 90 m (300 ft). They can remain submerged for as long as a few hours, possibly depending on temperature and degree of activity.

Huge aggregations of sea snakes have been reported. For example, in 1932 millions of *Astrotia stokesii*, a relative of *Pelamis*, were seen from a steamer in the Strait of Malacca, off the coast of Malaysia, and formed a line of snakes 3 m (9.8 ft) wide and 100 km (62 mi) long. The cause of this phenomenon is unknown, although it likely has to do with reproduction. In that same area, sea snakes can sometimes be seen swimming in schools of several dozen, and that after typhoons many dead specimens can be found on the beaches.

Feeding

Most sea snake species prey on fish, especially eels. The latter stiffens and dies within seconds, when bitten. One species prefers molluscs and crustaceans, such as prawns, while a few others feed only on fish eggs, which is unusual for a venomous snake. Some reef dwelling species have small heads and thin necks, making it possible for them to extract small eels from the soft bottom where they hide. Sea snakes will sometimes take bait from a fishing line.

Except for a single genus, all sea snakes are ovoviviparous; the young are born alive in the water where they live their entire life cycle. In some species, the young are quite large: up to half as long as the mother. The one exception is the genus *Laticauda*, which is oviparous; its five species all lay their eggs on land.

Venom

Like their cousins in the Elapidae family, the majority of sea snakes are highly venomous; however, when bites occur, it is rare for much venom to be injected, so that envenomation symptoms usually seem non-existent or trivial.

For example, *Pelamis platurus* has a venom more potent than any other terrestrial snake species in Costa Rica, but despite its abundance in the waters off its western coast, few human fatalities have been reported. Nevertheless, all sea snakes should be handled with great caution.

Bites in which envenomation does occur are usually painless and may not even be noticed when contact is made. Teeth may remain in the wound. There is usually little or no swelling, and it is rare for any nearby lymph nodes to be affected. The most important symptoms are rhabdomyolysis (rapid breakdown of skeletal muscle tissue) and paralysis. Early symptoms include headache, a thick-feeling tongue, thirst, sweating, and vomiting.

Symptoms that can occur after 30 minutes to several hours post-bite include generalized aching, stiffness, and tenderness of muscles all over the body. Passive stretching of the muscles is also painful, and trismus, which is similar to tetanus, is common. This is followed later on by symptoms typical of other elapid envenomations: a progressive flaccid paralysis, starting with ptosis and paralysis of voluntary muscles. Paralysis of muscles involved in swallowing and respiration can be fatal. After 3-8 hours, myoglobin as a result of muscle breakdown may start to show up in the blood plasma, which can cause the urine to turn a dark reddish, brown, or black colour, and eventually lead to acute renal failure. After 6 to 12 hours, severe hyperkalemia, also the result of muscle breakdown, can lead to cardiac arrest.

Sea snakes were at first regarded as a unified and separate family, the Hydrophiidae, that later came to comprise two subfamilies: the Hydrophiinae, or true/aquatic sea snakes (now 16 genera with 57 species), and the more primitive Laticaudinae, or sea kraits (1 genus, *Laticauda*, with 5 species).

Eventually, as it became clear just how closely related the sea snakes are to the elapids, the taxonomic situation became less well-defined. Some taxonomists responded by moving the sea snakes to the Elapidae, thereby creating the subfamilies Elapinae, Hydrophiinae and Laticaudinae, although the latter may be omitted if *Laticauda* is included in the Hydrophiinae.

No one has yet been able to convincingly work out the phylogenetic relationships between the various elapid subgroups, and the situation is still unclear. Therefore, others opted to either continue to work with the older traditional arrangements, if only for practical reasons, or to lump all of the genera together in the Elapidae, with no taxonomic subdivisions, to reflect the work that remains to be done.

At best, these snakes make difficult captives. Researcher described them as nervous and delicate captives that usually refuse to eat, preferring only to hide in the darkest corner of the tank. Over 50 years later, researcher wrote that although they were rarely displayed in western zoological parks, some species were regularly on display in Japanese aquariums.

Available food supply is one factor that limits the number of species that can be kept in captivity, since some have diets that are too specialized. Another is that some species appear too intolerant to handling, or even being removed from the water. Regarding their facilities, the *Laticauda* species need to be able to exit the water somewhere and bask, while the other strictly aquatic genera do not, basically requiring only a tank of filtered (synthetic) sea water maintained at about 29°C, along with a submerged shelter.

Species that have done relatively well in captivity include the ringed sea snake, *Hydrophis cyanocinctus*, which feed on fish and eels in particular. *Pelamis platurus* has done especially well in captivity, accepting small fish, including goldfish. However, care has to be taken to house them in round or oval tanks, or in rectangular tanks with corners that are well-rounded, to prevent the snakes from damaging their snouts by swimming into the sides.

Conservation Status

Most sea snakes are not on the CITES protection lists however, one species, *Laticauda crockeri*, is classified as vulnerable (Vu), another, *Aipysurus fuscus*, classified as endangered (En), and two, *Aipysurus foliosquama* and *Aipysurus apraefrontalis*, are classified as critically endangered (CE) according to the IUCN Red List of Threatened Species.

Sea Serpent

A sea serpent or sea dragon is a type of sea monster either wholly or partly serpentine.

Sightings of sea serpents have been reported for hundreds of years, and continue to be claimed today. Cryptozoologist Bruce Champagne identified more than 1200 purported sea serpent sightings. It is currently believed that the sightings can be best explained as known animals such as oarfish and whales.

Some cryptozoologists have suggested that the sea serpents are relict plesiosaurs, mosasaurs or other Mesozoic marine reptiles, an idea often associated with lake monsters such as the Loch Ness Monster.

In Norse mythology, *Jörmungandr*, or "Midgarðsormr" was a sea serpent so long that it encircled the entire world, Midgard. Some stories report of sailors mistaking its back for a chain of islands. Sea serpents also appear frequently in later Scandinavian folklore, particularly in that of Norway.

In 1028 CE, Saint Olaf killed and threw onto the mountain Syltefjellet in Valldal, Norway a sea serpent, the marks of which are still visible . In Swedish ecclesiastic and writer Olaus Magnus's *Carta marina*, many marine monsters of varied form, including an immense sea serpent, appear.

Moreover, in his 1555 work *History of the Northern Peoples*, Magnus gives the following description of a Norwegian sea serpent:

> *Those who sail up along the coast of Norway to trade or to fish, all tell the remarkable story of how a serpent of fearsome size, 200 feet long and 20 feet wide, resides in rifts and caves outside Bergen. On bright summer nights this serpent leaves the caves to eat calves, lambs and pigs, or it fares out to the sea and feeds on sea nettles, crabs and similar marine animals. It has ell-long hair hanging from its neck, sharp black scales and flaming red eyes. It attacks vessels, grabs and swallows people, as it lifts itself up like a column from the water.*

Sea serpents were known to sea-faring cultures in the Mediterranean and Near East, appearing in both mythology (the Babylonian Labbu) and in apparent eye-witness accounts (Aristotle's Historia Animalium). In the Aeneid, a pair of sea serpents killed Laocoön and his sons when Laocoön argued against bringing the Trojan Horse into Troy.

Sea serpent reported by Hans Egede, Bishop of Greenland, in 1734. Henry Lee suggested the giant squid as an explanation.

Hans Egede, the national saint of Greenland, gives an 18th century descriptions of a sea serpent. On 6 July 1734 his ship sailed past the coast of Greenland when suddenly those on board.

> *"Saw a most terrible creature, resembling nothing they saw before. The monster lifted its head so high that it seemed to be higher than the crow's nest on the mainmast. The head was small and the body short and wrinkled. The unknown creature was using giant fins which propelled it through the water. Later the sailors saw its tail as well. The monster was longer than our whole ship".*
>
> Egede. (Mareš, 1997)

Sea serpent sightings on the coast of New England, are documented beginning in 1638. An incident in August 1817 spawned a rather silly mix-up when a committee of the New England Linnaean Society went so far as to give a deformed terrestrial snake the name *Scoliophis atlanticus*, believing it was the juvenile form of a sea serpent that had recently been reported in Gloucester Harbor.

After the Linnaean Society's misidentification was discovered, it was frequently cited by debunkers as evidence that the creature did not exist.

A particularly famous sea serpent sighting was made by the men and officers of HMS *Daedalus* in August, 1848 during a voyage to Saint Helena in the South Atlantic; the creature they saw, some 60 feet (18 m) long, held a peculiar maned head above the water. The sighting caused quite a stir in the London papers, and Sir Richard Owen, the famous English biologist, proclaimed the beast an elephant seal. Other explanations for the sighting proposed that it was actually an upside-down canoe, or a posing giant squid.

Another sighting took place in 1905 off the coast of Brazil. The crew of the *Valhalla* and two naturalists, Michael J. Nicoll and E. G. B. Meade-Waldo, saw a long-necked, turtle headed creature, with a large dorsal fin. Based on its dorsal fin and the shape of its head, some (such as Heuvelmans) have suggested that the animal was some sort of marine mammal.

A skeptical suggestion is that the sighting was of a posing giant squid, but this is hard to accept given that squids do not swim with their fins or arms protruding from the water.

On April 25, 1977, the Japanese trawler Zuiyo Maru, sailing east of Christchurch, New Zealand, caught a strange, unknown creature in the trawl. Photographs and tissue specimens were taken. While initially identified as a prehistoric plesiosaur, analysis later indicated that the body was the carcass of a basking shark.

Skeptics and debunkers have questioned the interpretation of sea serpent sightings, suggesting that reports of serpents are misidentifications of things such as cetaceans (whales and dolphins), sea snakes, eels, basking sharks, baleen whales, oarfish, large pinnipeds, seaweed, driftwood, flocks of birds, and giant squid.

While most cryptozoologists recognize that at least some reports are simple misidentifications, they claim that many of the creatures described by those who have seen them look nothing like the known species put forward by skeptics and claim that certain reports stick out. For their part, the skeptics remain unconvinced, pointing out that even in the absence of out-right hoaxes, imagination has a way of twisting and inflating the slightly out-of-the-ordinary until it becomes extraordinary.

A recent posting on the Centre of Fortean Zoology (CFZ) blog by Cryptozoologist Dale Drinnon notes his check of the categories in Heuvelmans' In The Wake of the Sea-Serpents, in which he extracted the mistaken observation categories as a control to check the Sea-serpent categories by using the reports he created identikits for the mistaken observations and enlarged them to possibly 126 of Heuvelmans' sightings, making the mistaken observations the largest section of Heuvelmans' reports. His identikits include oarfish, basking sharks, toothed whales, baleen whales, lines of large whales for the largest Sea-serpent 'hump' sightings and trains of smaller cetaceans for the 'Many-finned', elephant seals and manta rays. Each of these categories was given a percentage of the whole body of reports, ranging between one per cent and 5 per cent with the whales at an average 2.5 per cent, figures which he considers comparable to the regular Sea-serpent categories of Super-eel and Marine Saurian (each of which he breaks into a larger and a smaller sized series following Heuvelmans' suggestion in In the Wake of the Sea-Serpents) Drinnon has also published in the 2010 CFZ yearbook in which he modifies Coleman's categories (below), adding a possible Giant otter category to the Giant Beavers and modifying several others, bringing the total to 17 categories to broaden the coverage. The broadened coverage allows more instances of conventional fishes such as sturgeons and catfishes, left off Coleman's list.

In a separate and earlier CFZ blog, Drinnon reviewed Bruce Champagne's sea-serpent categories and identified several of them as known animals, and several whales in particular Drinnon basically recognises the Longneck, Marine Saurian and Super-eel categories in this blog as well, with the modification that the Marine Saurian as spoken of by Champagne is more likely a large crocodile akin to *C. porosis* and that there has been a suggestion that an eel-like animal is involved in certain 'Many-finned' observations.

The whale categories he identifies are: BC 2A-Possible Odobenocetops, BC2B, Atlantic gray whale or Scrag Whale, BC 4B, as being similar to an unidentified large-finned beaked whale otherwise reported in the Pacific, and BC 5, the large Father-of-All-the-Turtles, as a humpback whale turned turtle.

Classification Systems

Cryptozoologists have argued for the existence of sea serpents by claiming that people report seeing similar things, and further arguing that it is possible to classify sightings into different "types". There have been different classification attempts with different results, although they share some common characteristics.

Anthonie Cornelis Oudemans

Megophias megophias: A large sea lion-like creature with a long neck and long tail. Over 200 feet (61 m) long. Only the male has a mane. It is cosmopolitan.

Bernard Heuvelmans

- *Long Necked* or *Megalotaria longicollis:* A 60-foot (18 m), long necked, short tailed sea lion. Hair and whiskers reported. Cosmopolitan.
- *Merhorse* or *Halshippus olai-magni:* A 60-foot (18 m), medium necked, large eyed, horse-headed pinniped. Often has whiskers. It is also cosmopolitan.
- 60-100-foot (18-30 m), medium necked, long bodied archaeocete. It has a series of humps or a crest on the spine like a sperm whale's or grey whale's. It only lives in the North Atlantic.
- *Super Otter* or *Hyperhydra egedei:* A 65-100-foot (20-30 m), medium necked, long bodied archeocete that resembles

an otter. It moves in numerous vertical undulations (6-7). Lived near Norway and Greenland, and presumed to be extinct by Heuvelmans.

- *Many Finned* or *Cetioscolopendra aeliani:* A 60-70-foot (18-21 m), short necked archeocete. It has a number of lateral projections that look like dorsal fins, but turned the incorrect way. Compare to the armor on *Desmatosuchus*, but much more prominent.
- *Super Eels:* A group of large and possibly unrelated eels. Partially based on the *Leptocephalus giganteus* larvae, later shown to be normal sized. Heuvelmans theorized eel, synbranchid, and elasmobranch identities as being possible. Cosmopolitan.
- *Marine Saurian:* A 50-60-foot (15-18 m) crocodile, or crocodile-like animal (Mosasaur, Pliosaur, etc.)
- *Yellow Belly:* A very large, 100-200-foot (30-61 m) yellow and black striped tadpole-shaped creature. Dropped.
- *Father-of-all-the-turtles:* A giant turtle. Dropped.
- *Giant Invertebrates:* Giant Venus's girdle and salp colonies. Added. It is not clear if Heuvelmans intended them to be unknown species or extreme forms of known species.

Loren Coleman and Patrick Huyghe

- *Classic Sea Serpent:* A quadrupedal, elongated animal with the appearance of many humps when swimming. Essentially a composite of the many humped, super otter, and super eels types. The authors suggest Basilosaurus as a candidate, or possibly Remingtoncetids.
- *Waterhorse:* A large pinniped, similar to the long necked and merhorse. Only the males are maned, but females appear to have snorkels. Both of their eyes are rather small. They are noteworthy for being behind both salt and fresh water sightings.
- *Mystery Cetacean:* A category of unknown whale species including double finned whales and dolphins, dorsal finned sperm whales, unknown beaked whales, an unknown orca, and others.

- *Giant Shark:* A surviving megalodon.
- *Mystery Manta:* A small manta ray with dorsal markings.
- *Great Sea Centipede:* Same as the many finned. The authors suggest the flippers may either be retractile, and the 'scaly' appearance could be caused by parasites.
- *Mystery Saurian:* Same as the marine saurian.
- *Cryptic Chelonian:* A resurrection of the father-of-all-turtles.
- *Mystery Sirenian:* Late surviving Steller's Sea Cow.
- *Giant Octopus, Octopus giganteus* or *Otoctopus giganteus:* A large cephalopod living in the tropical Atlantic.

Bruce Champagne

- *Long Necked:* A 30-foot (9.1 m) sea lion with a long neck and long tail. The neck is the same thickness or smaller than the head. Hair reported. It is capable of travel on land. Cosmopolitan.
- *Long Necked:* Similar to the above type but over 55 feet (17 m) long and far more robust. The neck is of lesser thickness than the head. Only inhabits water near Great Britain and Denmark.
- *Eel-Like:* A 20-30-foot (6.1-9.1 m) long heavily scaled or armored reptile. It is distinguished by a small square head with prominent tusks. 'Motorboating' behaviour on surface. Inhabits only the North Atlantic.
- *Eel-Like*: A 25-30-foot (7.6-9.1 m) beaked whale. It is distinguished by a tapering head and a dorsal crest. 'Motorboating' behaviour engaged in. Inhabits the Atlantic and Pacific. Possibly extinct.
- *Eel-Like:* A 60-70-foot (18-21 m), elongated reptile with no appendages. The head is very large and cow-like or reptilian with teeth similar to a crabeater seal's. Also shares the 'motorboating' behaviour. Inhabits the Atlantic, Pacific, and South China Sea. Possibly extinct.
- *Multi-Humped:* 30-60 feet (9.1-18 m) long. A possible reptile with a dorsal crest and the ability to move in several

undulations. The head has a distinctive 'cameloid' appearance. Identical with Cadborosaurus willsi.

- *Sailfin:* A 30-70-foot (9.1-21 m) beaked whale. It is distinguished by a very small head and a very large dorsal fin. Only found in the North West Atlantic. Possibly extinct.
- *Sailfin:* An elongated animal of possible mammalian or reptilian identity reported to be 12-85 feet (3.7-26 m) long. It has a long neck with a turtle-like head and a long continuous dorsal fin. Cosmopolitan.
- *Carapaced:* A large turtle or turtle-like creature (mammal) reported to be 10-45 feet (3.0-14 m) long. Carapace is described as jointed, segmented, and plated. May exhibit a dorsal crest of 'quills' and a type of oily hair. Cosmopolitan.
- *Saurian:* A large and occasionally spotted crocodile or crocodile-like creature up to 65 feet (20 m) long. Found in the Northern Atlantic and Mediterranean.
- *Segmented/Multi limbed:* An elongated mammalian creature up to 65 feet (20 m) long with the appearance of segmentation and many fins. Found in the Western Atlantic, Indian, and Pacific.

3 Scale Arrangements in Snakes

Snakes, like other reptiles, have a skin covered in scales. Snakes are entirely covered with scales or scutes of various shapes and sizes. Scales protect the body of the snake, aid it in locomotion, allow moisture to be retained within, alter the surface characteristics such as roughness to aid in camouflage, and in some cases even aid in prey capture (such as Acrochordus). The simple or complex colouration patterns (which help in camouflage and anti-predator display) are a property of the underlying skin, but the folded nature of scaled skin allows bright skin to be concealed between scales then revealed in order to startle predators.

Scales have been modified over time to serve other functions such as 'eyelash' fringes, and protective covers for the eyes with the most distinctive modification being the *rattle* of the North American rattlesnakes.

Snakes periodically moult their scaly skins and acquire new ones. This permits replacement of old worn out skin, disposal of parasites and is thought to allow the snake to grow. The arrangement of scales is used to identify snake species.

Snakes have been part and parcel of culture and religion. Vivid scale patterns have been thought to have influenced early art. The use of snake-skin in manufacture of purses, apparel and other articles led to large-scale killing of snakes, giving rise to advocacy for use of artificial snake-skin. Snake scales are also to be found as motifs in fiction, video games and films.

The scales of a snake primarily serve to reduce friction as it moves, since friction is the major source of energy loss in snake locomotion. The ventral (or belly) scales, which are large and oblong, are especially low-friction, and some arboreal species can use the edges to grip branches. Snake skin and scales help retain moisture in the animal's body. Snakes pick up vibrations from both the air and the ground, and can differentiate the two, using a complex system of internal resonances (perhaps involving the scales).

Snake scales are formed by the differentiation of the snake's underlying skin or epidermis. Each scale has an outer surface and an inner surface. The skin from the inner surface hinges back and forms a free area which overlaps the base of the next scale which emerges below this scale. A snake hatches with a fixed number of scales. The scales do not increase in number as the snake matures nor do they reduce in number over time. The scales however grow larger in size and may change shape with each moult.

Snakes have smaller scales around the mouth and sides of the body which allow expansion so that a snake can consume prey of much larger width than itself. Snake scales are made of keratin, the same material that hair and fingernails are made of. They are cool and dry to touch.

Snake scales are of different shapes and sizes. Snake scales may be granular, have a smooth surface or have a longitudinal ridge or keel on it. Often, snake scales have pits, tubercles and other fine structures which may be visible to the naked eye or under a microscope. Snake scales may be modified to form fringes, as in the case of the Eyelash Bush Viper, *Atheris ceratophora*, or rattles as in the case of the rattlesnakes of North America.

Certain primitive snakes such as boas, pythons and certain advanced snakes such as vipers have small scales arranged irregularly on the head. Other more advanced snakes have special large symmetrical scales on the head called *shields* or *plates*.

Snake scales occur in variety of shapes. They may be cycloid as in family.

Cycloid scales on *Leptotyphlops humilis* and other blind snake species are fluorescent, as a result when they are put under low frequency ultraviolet light (black light) they glow.

Typhlopidae, long and pointed with pointed tips, as in the case of the Green Vine Snake *Ahaetulla nasuta,* broad and leaf-like, as in the case of green pit vipers *Trimeresurus* spp or as broad as they are long, for example, as in Rat snake *Ptyas mucosus.*

In some cases, scales may be keeled weakly or strongly as in the case of the Buff-striped keelback *Amphiesma stolatum.* They may have bidentate tips as in some spp of *Natrix.* Some snakes, such as the Short Seasnake *Lapemis curtus,* may have spinelike and juxtaposed scales while others may have large and non-overlapping knobs as in the case of the Javan Mudsnake *Xenodermis javanicus.*

Another example of differentiation of snake scales is a transparent scale called the *brille* or *spectacle* which covers the eye of the snake. The brille is often referred to as a fused eyelid. It is shed as part of the old skin during moulting.

The most distinctive modification of the snake scale is the *rattle* of rattlesnakes, such as those of the genera *Crotalus* and *Sistrurus.* The rattle is made up of a series of loosely linked, interlocking chambers that when shaken, vibrate against one another to create the warning signal of a rattlesnake. Only the bottom button is firmly attached to the tip of the tail.

At birth, a rattlesnake hatchling has only a small button or 'primordial rattle' which is firmly attached to the tip of the tail. The first segment is added when the hatchling sheds its skin for the first time. A new section is added each time the skin is shed until a rattle is formed. The rattle grows as the snake ages but segments are also prone to breaking off and hence the length of a rattle is not a reliable indicator of the age of a snake.

Scales, more specifically, mostly consist of hard beta keratins which are basically transparent. The colours of the scale are due to pigments in the inner layers of the skin and not due to the scale material itself. Scales are hued for all colours in this manner except for blue and green. Blue is caused by the ultrastructure of the scales. By itself, such a scale surface diffracts light and gives a blue hue, while, in combination with yellow from the inner skin it gives a beautiful iridescent green.

Some snakes have the ability to change the hue of their scales slowly. This is typically seen in cases where the snake becomes lighter or darker with change in season. In some cases, this change may take place between day and night.

The shedding of scales is called *ecdysis*, or, in normal usage *moulting* or *sloughing*. In the case of snakes, the complete outer layer of skin is shed in one layer. Snake scales are not discrete but extensions of the epidermis hence they are not shed separately, but are ejected as a complete contiguous outer layer of skin during each moult, akin to a sock being turned inside out.

Moulting serves a number of functions - firstly, the old and worn skin is replaced, secondly, it helps get rid of parasites such as mites and ticks. Renewal of the skin by moulting is supposed to allow growth in some animals such as insects, however this view has been disputed in the case of snakes.

Moulting is repeated periodically throughout a snake's life. Before a moult, the snake stops eating and often hides or moves to a safe place. Just before shedding, the skin becomes dull and dry looking and the eyes become cloudy or blue-coloured. The inner surface of the old outer skin liquefies. This causes the old outer skin to separate from the new inner skin. After a few days, the eyes clear and the snake "crawls" out of its old skin. The old skin breaks near the mouth and the snake wriggles out aided by rubbing against rough surfaces. In many cases the cast skin peels backward over the body from head to tail, in one piece like an old sock. A new, larger, and brighter layer of skin has formed underneath.

An older snake may shed its skin only once or twice a year, but a younger, still-growing snake, may shed up to four times a year. The discarded skin gives a perfect imprint of the scale pattern and it is usually possible to identify the snake if this discard is reasonably complete and intact.

Scale arrangements are important, not only for taxonomic utility, but also for forensic reasons and conservation of snake species. Excepting for the head, snakes have imbricate scales, overlapping like the tiles on a roof. Snakes have rows of scales along the whole or part of their length and also many other specialised scales, either singly or in pairs, occurring on the head and other regions of the body.

The dorsal (or body) scales on the snake's body are arranged in rows along the length of their bodies. Adjacent rows are diagonally offset from each other. Most snakes have an odd number of rows across the body though certain species have an even number of rows e.g. *Zaocys* spp. In the case of some aquatic and marine snakes, the scales are granular and the rows cannot be counted.

The number of rows range from ten in Tiger Ratsnake *Spilotes pullatus*; thirteen in *Dryocalamus*, *Liopeltis*, *Calamaria* and Asian coral snakes of genus *Calliophis*; 65 to 75 in pythons; 74 to 93 in *Kolpophis* and 130 to 150 in *Acrochordus*. The majority of the largest family of snakes, the *Colubridae* have 15, 17 or 19 rows of scales. The maximum number of rows are in mid-body and they reduce in count towards the head and on the tail.

Identification of cephalic scales is most conveniently begun with reference to the nostril which is easily identified on the snake. There are two scales enclosing the nostril which are called the nasals. In colubrids, the nostril lies between the nasals while in vipers it lies in the centre of a single nasal scale. The outer nasal (near the snout) is called the prenasal while the inner nasal (near the eye) is called the postnasal. Along the top of the snout connecting the nasals on both sides of the head are scales called internasals. Between the two prenasals is a scale at the tip of the snout called the rostral scale.

The scales around the eye are called circumorbital scales and are named as 'ocular' scales but with appropriate prefix. The ocular scale proper is a transparent scale covering the eye which is called the spectacle, brille or eyecap. The circumorbital scales towards the snout or the front are called preocular scales, those towards the rear are called postocular scales and those towards the upper or dorsal side are called as supraocular scales. Circumorbital scales towards the ventral or lower side, if any, are called as subocular scales. Between the preocular and the postnasal scales are one or two scales called as loreal scales. Loreal scales are absent in elapids.

The scales along the lips of the snake are called as labials. Those on the upper lip are called supralabials while those on the lower labial are called infralabials. Between the eyeballs on top of the head, adjacent to the supraoculars are the frontal scales. The prefrontal scales are the scales connected to the frontals towards the tip of the snout which are in contact with the internasals. They may have a scale in between them. The back of the top of the head has scales connected to the frontal scales called as the parietal scales. At the sides of the back of the head between the parietals above and the supralabials below are scales called temporal scales.

Part of the body of a snake having yellow and black rings. The body is triangular in section and has a prominent line of scales on the apical vertebral ridge.

On the underside of the head, a snake has an anterior scale called as the mental scale. Connected to the mental scales and all along the lower jaws are the infralabials. Along the lower jaw connected to infralabials are a pair of shields called the anterior chin shields. Next to the anterior chin shields, further back along the jaw are another pair of shields called the posterior chin shields. In some texts the chinshields are referred to as *submaxillary* scales.

Scales in the central or *throat* region, which are in contact with the first ventral scales of a snake's body and are flanked by the chin shields, are called gular scales. The mental groove is a longitudinal groove on the underside of the head between large, paired chin shields and smaller gular scales.

Body Scales

The scales on the body of the snake are called the dorsal or costal scales. Sometimes there is a special row of large scales along the top of the back of the snake, i.e., the uppermost row, called the vertebral scales. The enlarged scales on the belly of the snake are called ventral scales or gastrosteges. The number of ventral scales can be a guide to the species. In 'advanced' (Caenophidian) snakes, the broad belly scales and rows of dorsal scales correspond to the vertebrae, allowing scientists to count the vertebrae without dissection.

Tail Scales

At the end of the ventral scales of the snake is an anal plate which protects the opening to the cloaca (a shared opening for waste and reproductive material to pass) on the underside near the tail. This anal scale may be single or divided into a pair. The part of the body beyond the anal scale is considered to be the tail.

Sometimes snakes have enlarged scales, either single or paired, under the tail; these are called subcaudals or urosteges. These subcaudals may be smooth or keeled as in *Bitis arietans somalica*. The end of the tail may simply taper into a tip (as in the case of most snakes), it may form a spine (as in *Acanthophis*), end in a bony spur (as in *Lachesis*), a rattle (as in *Crotalus*), or a rudder as seen in many sea snakes.

Sources. Details for this section have been sourced from scale diagrams in Malcolm Smith. Details of scales of Buff-striped Keelback have been taken from Daniels.

Scales do not play an important role in distinguishing between the families but are important at generic and specific level. There is an elaborate scheme of nomenclature of scales. Scales patterns, by way of scale surface or texture, pattern and colouration and the division of the anal plate, in combination with other morphological characteristics, are the principal means of classifying snakes down to species level.

In certain areas in North America, where the diversity of snakes is not too large, easy keys based on simple identification of scales have been devised for the lay public to distinguish poisonous snakes from non-poisonous snakes. In other places with large biodiversity, such as Myanmar, publications caution that venomous and non-venomous snakes cannot be easily distinguished apart without careful examination.

The scales patterning may also be used for individual identification in field studies. Clipping of specific scales, such as the subcaudals, to mark individual snakes is a popular approach to population estimation by mark and recapture techniques.

There is no simple way of differentiating a venomous snake from a non-venomous one merely by using a scale character. Finding out whether a snake is venomous or not is correctly done by identification of the species of a snake with the help of experts, or in their absence, close examination of the snake and using authoritative references on the snakes of the particular geographical region to identify it. Scale patterns help to indicate the species and from the references, it can be verified if the snake species is known to be venomous or not.

Species identification using scales requires a fair degree of knowledge about snakes, their taxonomy, snake-scale nomenclature as well as familiarity with and access to scientific literature. Distinguishing by using scale diagrams whether a snake is venomous or not in the field cannot be done in the case of uncaught specimens. It is not advisable to catch a snake to check whether it is venomous or not using scale diagrams. Most books or websites provide an array of traits of the local herpetofauna, other than scale diagrams, which help to distinguish whether a snake in the field is venomous or not.

In certain regions, presence or absence of certain scales may be a quick way to distinguish non-venomous and venomous snakes, but used with care and knowledge of exceptions. For example, in Myanmar, the presence or absence of loreal scales can be used to distinguish between relatively harmless Colubrids and lethally venomous Elapids. The rule of hand for this region is that the absence of a loreal scale between the nasal scale and pre-ocular scale indicates that the snake is an Elapid and hence lethal. This rule-of-thumb cannot be used without care as it cannot be applied to vipers, which have a large number of small scales on the head. A careful check would also be needed to exclude known poisonous members of the Colubrid family such as *Rhabdophis*.

In South Asia, it is advisable to take the snake which has bitten a person, if it has been killed, and carry it along to the hospital for possible identification by medical staff using scale diagrams so that an informed decision can be taken them as to whether and which anti-venom is to be administered. However, attempts to catch it or kill the venomous snake are not advised as the snake may bite more people.

Cultural Significance

Snakes have been a motif in human culture and religion and an object of dread and fascination all over the world. The vivid patterns of snake scales, such as the Gaboon Viper, both repel and fascinate the human mind. Such patterns have inspired dread and awe in humans from pre-historic times and these can be seen in the art prevalent to those times. Studies of fear imagery and psychological arousal indicate that snake scales are a vital component of snake imagery. Snake scales also appear to have affected Islamic art in the form of tessallated mosaic patterns which show great similarity to snake-scale patterns.

Snakeskin, with its highly periodic cross-hatch or grid patterns, appeals to people's aesthetics and have been used to manufacture many leather articles including fashionable accessories. The use of snakeskin has however endangered snake populations and resulted in international restrictions in trade of certain snake species and populations in the form of CITES provisions. Animal lovers in many countries now propagate the use of artificial snakeskin instead, which are easily produced from embossed leather, patterned fabric, plastics and other materials.

Snake scales occur as a motif regularly in computer action games. A snake scale was portrayed as a clue in the 1982 film *Blade Runner*. Snake scales also figure in popular fiction, such as the Harry Potter series (desiccated Boomslang skin is used as a raw material for concocting the Polyjuice potion), and also in teen fiction.

4 Snake Venom

Snake venom is highly modified saliva that is produced by special glands of certain species of snakes. The gland which secretes the zootoxin is a modification of the parotid salivary gland of other vertebrates, and is usually situated on each side of the head below and behind the eye, invested in a muscular sheath. It is provided with a large alveoli in which the venom is stored before being conveyed by a duct to the base of the channeled or tubular fang through which it is ejected. Snake venom is a combination of many different proteins and enzymes. Many of these proteins are harmless to humans, but some are toxins.

Snake venoms are generally not dangerous when ingested, and are therefore not technically poisons.

Chemistry

Snake venom consists of proteins, enzymes, substances with a cytotoxic effect, neurotoxins and coagulants.

Phosphodiesterases are used to interfere with the prey's cardiac system, mainly to lower the blood pressure.

Phospholipase A2 causes hemolysis by lysing the phospholipid cell membranes of red blood cells.

Snake venom inhibits cholinesterase to make the prey lose muscle control.

Hyaluronidase increases tissue permeability to increase the rate that other enzymes are absorbed into the prey's tissues.

Amino acid oxidases and proteases are used for digestion. Amino acid oxidase also triggers some other enzymes and is responsible for the yellow colour of the venom of some species.

Snake venom often contains ATPase, an enzyme which catalyzes the hydrolysis of ATP to ADP and a free phosphate ion, or to AMP and diphosphate.

Snake toxins have a great variety in their function. The two major families are neurotoxins (those that attack the nervous system) and cytotoxins (those that attack cells). They can be further subdivided as follows:

- Neurotoxins
- Fasciculins
- Dendrotoxins
- a-neurotoxins
- Cytotoxins
- Phospholipases
- Cardiotoxins
- Haemotoxins

The beginning of a new impulse:

(a) An exchange of ions (charged atoms) across the nerve cell membrane sends a depolarising current towards the end of the nerve cell (cell terminus).

(b) When the depolarising current arrives at the nerve cell terminus, the neurotransmitter acetylcholine (ACh), which is held in vesicles, is released into the space between the two nerves (synapse). It moves across the synapse to the postsynaptic receptors.

(c) If ACh remains at the receptor, the nerve stays stimulated, causing incontrollable muscle contractions. This condition is called tetany. So an enzyme called acetylcholinesterase destroys the ACh so tetany does not occur.

Fasciculins

These toxins attack cholinergic neurons (those that use ACh as a transmitter) by destroying acetylcholinesterase (AChE). ACh therefore cannot be broken down and stays in the receptor. This causes tetany, which can lead to death.

Dendrotoxins

Dendrotoxins inhibit neurotransmissions by blocking the exchange of positive and negative ions across the neuronal membrane lead to no nerve impulse. So it paralyses the nerves.

α-neurotoxins

α-neurotoxins also attack cholinergic neurons. They mimic the shape of the acetylcholine molecule and therefore fit into the receptors → they block the ACh flow → feeling of numbness and paralysis.

Snake examples:

- Kraits use erabutoxin (the Many-banded krait uses Bungarotoxin)
- Cobras use cobratoxin,

Cytotoxins

Phospholipases

Phospholipase is an enzyme that transforms the phospholipid molecule into a lysophospholipid (soap) ==> the new molecule attracts and binds fat and rips a hole in the cell membrane. Consequently water flows into the cell and destroys the molecules in it. That is called necrosis.

Cardiotoxins

Actually cardiotoxins are muscle venoms. They bind to particular sites on the surface of muscle cells causing depolarisation ==> the toxin prevents muscle contraction. For example the heart muscle: the heart will beat irregularly and stop beating, which will cause death.

Haemotoxins

The toxin destroys red blood cells (erythrocytes). This symptom is called haemolysis. As it is a very slowly progressing venom it would probably not kill a human - another toxin in the snake's venom would most certainly have caused death by then.

List of snake venom toxins:

- Piscivorin from the Eastern Cottonmouth
- Triflin from the Habu snake

- Ophanin from the King Cobra
- Latisemin from the Erabu snake
- Ablomin from the Mamushi snake

Evolution

The presence of enzymes in snake venom has led to the belief that it was an adaptation to assist in the digestion of prey, but, studies of the western diamondback rattlesnake, a snake with highly proteolytic venom, show that envenomation has no impact on the time food takes to pass through the gut. More research is needed to determine the selective pressures that have armed snakes in this way.

Injection

Vipers

In the vipers, which furnish examples of the most highly developed venom delivery apparatus, although inferior to some in its toxic effects, the venom gland is very large and in intimate relation with the masseter or temporal muscle, consisting of two bands, the superior arising from behind the eye, the inferior extending from the gland to the mandible. A groove or duct can be located traveling from the modified salivary glands where venom is produced down the length of the fang and out to the tip. In some species, notably the vipers and cobras, this groove is completely closed over. In other species, such as the adders and mambas, this groove is not covered, or only covered partially. From the anterior extremity of the gland the duct passes below the eye and above the maxillary bone, where it makes a bend, to the basal orifice of the venom fang, which is ensheathed in a thick fold of mucous membrane, the vagina dentis. By means of the movable maxillary bone hinged to the prefrontal, and connected with the tranverse bone which is pushed forward by muscles set in action by the opening of the mouth, the tubular fang is erected and the venom discharged through the distal orifice in which it terminates. When the snake bites, the jaws close up, causing the gland to be powerfully wrung, and the venom pressed out into the duct.

Elapids

In the proteroglyphous elapids, the fangs are tubular, but are short and do not possess the mobility seen in vipers.

Colubrids

In many opisthoglyphous colubrids, with grooved teeth situated at the posterior extremity of the maxilla, a small posterior portion of the upper labial or salivary gland is converted into a venom-secreting organ, distinguished by a light yellow colour, provided with a duct larger than any of those of the labial gland, and proceeding inward and downward to the base of the grooved fang; the duct is not in direct connection with the groove, but the two communicate through the mediation of the cavity enclosed by the folds of mucous membrane surrounding the tooth, and united in front.

The reserve or successional teeth, which are always present just behind or on the side of the functional fang of all venomous snakes, are in no way connected with the duct until called upon to replace a fang that has been lost. It could not be otherwise, since the duct would require a new terminal portion for each new fang; and as the replacement takes place alternately from two parallel series, the new venom-conveying tooth does not occupy exactly the same position as its predecessor.

Two genera, *Doliophis* among the elapids and *Causus* among the viperids, are highly remarkable for having the venom gland and its duct of a great length, extending along each side of the body and terminating in front of the heart. Instead of the muscles of the temporal region serving to press out the venom into the duct, this action is performed by those of the side of the body.

When biting, a viperid snake merely strikes, discharging the venom the moment the fangs penetrate the skin, and then immediately lets it go. A proteroglyph or opisthoglyph, on the contrary, closes its jaws like a dog on the part bitten, often holding on firmly for a considerable time. The venom, which is mostly a clear, limpid fluid of a pale straw or amber colour, or rarely greenish, sometimes with a certain amount of suspended matter, is exhausted after several bites, and the glands have to recuperate.

Mechanics of Spitting

Venom can be ejected otherwise than by a bite, as in the so-called spitting cobras of the genera *Naja* and *Hemachatus*. Some of these deadly snakes, when irritated, are capable of shooting venom from the mouth, at a distance of 4 to 8 feet. These snakes' fangs have been modified for the purposes of spitting: inside the fangs of a spitting cobra is a channel which makes a ninety degree bend to the lower front of the fang. When the snake is threatened the muscles of the venom gland squeeze the venom sac and as a result venom is projected forward. Spitters may spit thirty or forty times in succession, and even then the snake is still able to deliver a fatal bite.

Spitting is a defensive reaction only. The snake tends to aim for the eyes of a perceived threat; a direct hit can cause temporary shock and blindness through severe inflammation of the cornea and conjunctiva. While there are no serious results if the venom is washed away at once with plenty of water, the blindness caused by a successful spit can become permanent if left untreated. Contact with the skin is not in itself dangerous, but open wounds may become envenomated.

Some Effects

There are four distinct types of venom that act on the body differently.

1. *Proteolytic venom* dismantles the molecular structure of the area surrounding and including the bite.
2. *Hemotoxic venoms* act on the heart and cardiovascular system.
3. *Neurotoxic venom* acts on the nervous system and brain.
4. *Cytotoxic venom* has a localized action at the site of the bite.

It is noteworthy that the size of the venom fangs is in no relation to the virulence of the venom. The comparatively innocent Indo-Malay Lachesis alluded to above have enormous fangs, whilst the smallest fangs are found in the Hydrophids which possess very potent venom.

Proteroglyphous Snakes

The effect of the venom of proteroglyphous snakes (*Hydrophids, Bungarus, Dendroaspis, Elaps, Pseudechis, Notechis, Acanthophis*) is mainly on the nervous system, respiratory paralysis being quickly produced by bringing the venom into contact with the central nervous mechanism which controls respiration; the pain and local swelling which follow a bite are not usually severe.

The bite of all the proteroglyphous elapids, even of the smallest and gentlest, such as the *Elaps* or coral snakes, is, so far as known, deadly to humans.

Vipers

Viper venom (*Daboia, Echis, Lachesis, Crotalus*) acts more on the vascular system, bringing about coagulation of the blood and clotting of the pulmonary arteries; its action on the nervous system is not great, no individual group of nerve-cells appears to be picked out, and the effect upon respiration is not so direct; the influence upon the circulation explains the great depression which is a symptom of viperine envenomation. The pain of the wound is severe, and is speedily followed by swelling and discolouration. The symptoms produced by the bite of the European vipers are thus described by the best authorities on snake venom (Martin and Lamb):

> The bite is immediately followed by local pain of a burning character; the limb soon swells and becomes discoloured, and within one to three hours great prostration, accompanied by vomiting, and often diarrhoea, sets in. Cold, clammy perspiration is usual. The pulse becomes extremely feeble, and slight dyspnoea and restlessness may be seen. In severe cases, which occur mostly in children, the pulse may become imperceptible and the extremities cold; the patient may pass into coma. In from twelve to twenty-four hours these severe constitutional

symptoms usually pass off; but in the meantime the swelling and discolouration have spread enormously. The limb becomes phlegmonous, and occasionally suppurates. Within a few days recovery usually occurs somewhat suddenly, but death may result from the severe depression or from the secondary effects of suppuration. That cases of death, in adults as well as in children, are not infrequent in some parts of the Continent is mentioned in the last chapter of this Introduction.

The Viperidae differ much among themselves in the toxicity of their venom. Some, such as the Indian *Daboia russelli* and *Echis carinatus*; the American vipers *Crotalus*, *Lachesis muta* and *Bothrops lanceolatus*; and the African *Causus*, *Bitis*, and *Cerastes*, cause fatal results unless a remedy is speedily applied. On the other hand, the Indian and Malay *Lachesis* seldom cause the death of humans, their bite in some instances being no worse than the sting of a hornet. The bite of the larger European vipers may be very dangerous, and followed by fatal results, especially in children, at least in the hotter parts of the Continent; whilst the small *Vipera ursinii*, which hardly ever bites unless roughly handled, does not seem to be possessed of a very virulent venom, and, although very common in some parts of Austria-Hungary, is not known to have ever caused a serious accident.

Opisthoglyphous Colubrids

Biologists had long known that some snakes had rear fangs, 'inferior' venom injection mechanisms that might immobilize prey; although a few fatalities were on record, until 1957 the possibility that such snakes were deadly to humans seemed at most remote. The deaths of two prominent herpetologists from African colubrid bites changed that assessment, and recent events reveal that several other species of rear-fanged snakes have venoms that are potentially lethal to large vertebrates.

Boomslang and vine snake venom are toxic to blood cells and thin the blood (hemotoxic, hemorrhagic). Early symptoms include headaches, nausea, diarrhea, lethargy, mental disorientation, bruising and bleeding at the site and all body openings. Exsanguination is the main cause of death from such a bite.

The Groen Boomslang's venom is the most potent of all rear-fanged snakes in the world. Although it has venom more potent that many vipers and some elapids, it causes fewer fatalities. This is because the Groen Boomslang only secretes a small amount of venom when it bites and compared to the more aggressive Black Mamba it is much less aggressive.

Symptoms of a bite from these snakes are nausea and internal bleeding, and one could die from a brain hemorrhage and respiratory collapse.

Aglyphous Snakes

Experiments made with the secretion of the parotid gland of *Tropidonotus* and *Zamenis* have shown that even aglyphous snakes are not entirely devoid of venom, and point to the conclusion that the physiological difference between so-called harmless and venomous snakes is only one of degree, just as there are various steps in the transformation of an ordinary parotid gland into a venom gland or of a solid tooth into a tubular or grooved fang.

Immunity

Among Snakes

The question whether individual snakes are immune to their own venom is not yet definitely settled, though there is a known example of a cobra which self-envenomated, resulting in a large abscess requiring surgical intervention but showing none of the other effects that would have proven rapidly lethal in prey species or humans. Furthermore, certain harmless species, such as the North American *Coronella getula* and the Brazilian *Rhacidelus brazili*, are proof against the venom of the crotalines which frequent the same districts, and which they are able to overpower and feed upon. The Tropical Rat Snake, *Spilotes variabilis*, is the enemy of the Fer-de-lance in St. Lucia, and it is said that in their encounters the Cribo is invariably the victor. Repeated experiments have shown the

European Common Snake, *Tropidonotus natrix*, not to be affected by the bite of *Vipera berus* and *Vipera aspis*, this being due to the presence, in the blood of the harmless snake, of toxic principles secreted by the parotid and labial glands, and analogous to those of the venom of these vipers. Several North American species of Rat snakes as well as King snakes have proven to be immune or highly resistant to the venom of Rattle snake species.

Among Other Animals

The Hedgehog, the Mongoose, the Honey Badger, the Secretary Bird and a few other birds feeding on snakes, are known to be immune to an ordinary dose of snake venom; whether the pig may be considered so is still uncertain, although it is well known that, owing to its subcutaneous layer of fat, it is often bitten without ill effect. The garden dormouse (*Eliomys quercinus*) has recently been added to the list of animals refractory to viper venom. Some populations of California Ground Squirrel are at least partially immune to Rattlesnake venom as adults.

Among Humans

The acquisition of human immunity against snake venom is one of the oldest forms of vaccinology known to date (about AD 60, Psylli Tribe). Since then many humans have attempted to inoculate themselves with snake venom in order to achieve immunity. Charles Tanner and Herschel Flowers studied with dried snake venom and achieved strong immunity. Joel La Rocque self injected Eastern diamondback venom and developed a high IgG neutralizing antibody for several rattlesnake species. Harold Mierkey has done so for years. Tim Friede has studied twice with a self-directed vaccine experiment using pure venom and achieved very high IgG neutralizing antibodies with mamba and cobra venom. The present goal is to develop a DNA-based vaccine for the Old World using the genes that encode the venom with an electroporation device for DNA delivery . If successful, some of the over 100,000 people that die each year from snakebite in the Old World will be saved.

Traditional Treatment

The subject of snake venoms is one which has always attracted much attention and which has made great progress within the last quarter of a century. Plants used to treat snakebites in Trinidad and Tobago are made into tinctures with alcohol or olive oil and kept in rum flasks called 'snake bottles'. Snakes bottles contain several different plants and/ or insects.

The plants used include the vine called monkey ladder (*Bauhinia cumanensis* or *Bauhinia excisa*, Fabaceae) is pounded and put on the bite. Alternatively a tincture is made with a piece of the vine and kept in a snake bottle. Other plants used include: mat root (*Aristolochia rugosa*), cat's claw (*Pithocellobium unguis-cati*), tobacco (*Nicotiana tabacum*), snake bush (*Barleria lupulina*), obie seed (*Cola nitida*), and wild gri gri root (*Acrocomia ierensis*). Some snake bottles also contain the caterpillars (*Battus polydamus*, Papilionidae) that eat tree leaves (*Aristolochia trilobata*). Emergency snake medicines are obtained by chewing a three-inch piece of the root of bois canôt (*Cecropia peltata*) and administering this chewed-root solution to the bitten(usually hunting dogs). This is a common native plant of Latin America and the Caribbean which makes it appropriate as an emergency remedy. Another native plant used is mardi gras (*Renealmia alpinia*) (berries), which are crushed together with the juice of wild cane (*Costus scaber*) and given to the bitten. Quick fixes have included applying chewed tobacco from cigarettes, cigars or pipes as well. Making cuts around the puncture or sucking out the venom has also been helpful.

Serotherapy

Especially noteworthy is progress regarding the defensive reaction by which the blood may be rendered proof against their effect, by processes similar to vaccination—antipoisonous serotherapy.

The studies to which we allude have not only conduced to a method of treatment against snake-bites, but have thrown a new light on the great problem of immunity.

They have shown that the antitoxic sera do not act as chemical antidotes in destroying the venom, but as physiological antidotes; that, in addition to the venom glands, snakes possess other glands supplying their blood with substances antagonistic to the venom, such as also exist in various animals refractory to snake venom, the hedgehog and the mongoose for instance.

Regional Venom Specificity

Unfortunately, the specificity of the different snake venoms is such that, even when the physiological action appears identical, serum injections or graduated direct inoculations confer immunity towards one species or a few allied species only.

Thus, a European in Australia who had become immune to the venom of the deadly Australian Tiger Snake, *Notechis scutatus*, manipulating these snakes with impunity, and was under the impression that his immunity extended also to other species, when bitten by a *Denisonia superba*, an allied elapine, died the following day.

In India, the serum prepared with the venom of *Naja tripudians* has been found to be without effect on the venom of the two species of kraits of the genus *Bungarus*, and the Old World vipers *Daboia russelli* and *Echis carinatus*, and the pit viper *Trimeresurus popeiorum*. *Daboia russelli* serum is without effect on colubrine venoms, or those of *Echis* and *Trimeresurus*.

In Brazil, serum prepared with the venom of the New World pit viper *Lachesis lanceolatus* is without action on *Crotalus* venom.

Antivenom snakebite treatment must be matched as the type of envenomation that has occurred.

In the Americas, polyvalent antivenoms are available that are effective against the bites of most pit vipers.

These are not effective against coral snake envenomation, which requires a specific antivenom to their neurotoxic venom.

The situation is even more complex in countries like India, with its rich mix of vipers (family Viperidae) and highly neurotoxic cobras and kraits of the family Elapidae.

Venomous Snake

Venomous snakes are snakes which have venom glands and specialized teeth for the injection of venom. Members of the families Elapidae, Viperidae and Atractaspididae (and some from Colubridae as well) are major venomous snakes.

Venomous snakes use modified saliva, snake venom, usually delivered through highly specialized teeth such as hollow fangs, for the purpose of prey immobilization and self-defense. In contrast, non-venomous species either constrict their prey, or simply overpower it with their jaws.

Venomous snakes include several families of snakes and do not form a single taxonomic group. This has been interpreted to mean that venom in snakes originated more than once as the result of convergent evolution.

Evidence has recently been presented for the Toxicofera hypothesis however; venom was present (in small amounts) in the ancestor of all snakes (as well as several lizard families) as 'toxic saliva' and evolved to extremes in those snake families normally classified as venomous by parallel evolution. The Toxicofera hypothesis further implies that 'non venomous' snake lineages have either lost the ability to produce venom (but may still have lingering venom pseudogenes), or actually do produce venom in small quantities, likely sufficient to assist in small prey capture, but cause no harm to humans if bitten.

Lists or rankings of the world's "most venomous snakes" are tentative and differ greatly due to numerous factors, including the recentness and reliability of the data, the number of species analyzed, and the testing methods used.

In addition, since mice are the common indicator used to test venom from venomous snakes in LD_{50} test, the LD_{50} results may not reflect the actual effects on humans due to the physiological differences between mice and humans. For example, many venomous snakes are specialized predators on mice, their venom may be adapted specifically to incapacitate mice. While most mammals have a very similar physiology, LD_{50} results may or may not be directly relevant to humans.

Moreover, in terms of many other factors, the most venomous species may not always be the most dangerous; for example, while the Russell's viper, the Saw-scaled viper, the King cobra and the Black mamba have a significantly weaker venom than the Inland taipan, the prior two are responsible for far more deaths due to various factors (such as their wide distributions and inconspicuous appearance), while the latter two cause higher mortality rates and a faster death time in humans due to their high attack position and large dose of highly potent venom delivered.

While there have been numerous studies on snake venom, potency estimates can vary, creating overlap and greatly complicating the task. Further, LD_{50} may be measured through intramuscular, intraperitoneal, intravenous or subcutaneous injections on small rodents, although the latter is the most applicable to actual bites.

It should also be considered that mice, the most commonly used animals in determining LD_{50}, may react to some snake venoms differently than humans do. Thus, it remains difficult to compile such lists.

Many of these lists only take into account of terrestrial and arboreal snakes and neglect to list the of venom of the sea snakes. Species of sea snakes have been listed to have more toxic venom than even that of the inland taipan and further investigations of some species' venom are needed.

Other Information

Venomous snakes are often said to be poisonous, although this is not the correct term, as venoms and poisons are different. Poisons can be absorbed by the body, such as through the skin or digestive system, while venoms must first be introduced directly into tissues or the blood stream (envenomated) through mechanical means. It is, for example, therefore harmless to drink snake venom as long as there are no lacerations inside the mouth or digestive tract.

There are however two exceptions: the *Rhabdophis* snakes (keelback snakes) secrete poison from glands that it gets from the poisonous toads that it preys on; similarly certain garter snakes from Oregon retain toxins in their liver from the newts they eat.

Families of Venomous Snakes

Over 600 species are known to be venomous—about a quarter of all snake species. The following table lists some major species:

- Family
- Atractaspididae (atractaspidids)
- Burrowing asps, mole vipers, stiletto snakes.
- Colubridae (colubrids)

Most are harmless, but others have toxic saliva and at least five species, including the boomslang (*Dispholidus typus*), have caused human fatalities.

Elapidae (elapids)

Sea snakes, Taipans, Brown snakes, Coral snakes, Kraits, King Cobra, Mambas, Cobras.

Viperidae (viperids)

True vipers and pit vipers, including rattlesnakes and copperheads and cottonmouths.

5 Wave-like Movement of Snakes

Undulatory locomotion is the type of motion characterized by wave-like movement patterns that act to propel an animal forward. Examples of this type of gait include crawling in snakes, or swimming in the lamprey. Although this is typically the type of gait utilized by limbless animals, some creatures with limbs, such as the salamander, choose to forgo use of their legs in certain environments and exhibit undulatory locomotion. This movement strategy is important to study in order to create novel robotic devices capable of traversing a variety of environments.

In limbless locomotion, forward locomotion is generated by propagating flexural waves along the length of the animal's body. Forces generated between the animal and surrounding environment lead to a generation of alternating sideways forces that act to move the animal forward. These forces generate thrust and drag.

Hydrodynamics

Simulation predicts that thrust and drag are dominated by viscous forces at low Reynolds numbers and inertial forces at higher Reynolds numbers. When swimming in a fluid two main forces are thought to play a role:

1. *Skin Friction:* Generated due to the resistance of a fluid to shearing and is proportional to speed of the flow. This dominates undulatory swimming in spermatozoa and the nematode.

2. *Form Force:* Generated by the differences in pressure on the surface of the body and it varies with the square of flow speed.

At low Reynolds number (Re~10^0), skin friction accounts for nearly all of the thrust and drag. For those animals which undulate at intermediate Reynolds number (Re~10^1), such as the Ascidian larvae, both skin friction and form force account for the production of drag and thrust. At high Reynolds number (Re~10^2), both skin friction and form force act to generate drag, but only form force produces thrust.

Kinematics

In animals that move without use of limbs, the most common feature of the locomotion is a rostral to caudal wave that travels down their body. However, this pattern can change based on the particular undulating animal, the environment, and the metric in which the animal is optimizing (i.e. speed, energy, etc.). The most common mode of motion is simple undulations in which lateral bending is propagated from head to tail.

Snakes can exhibit five different modes of terrestrial locomotion:

1. lateral undulation;
2. sidewinding;
3. concertina;
4. rectilinear; and
5. slide-pushing.

Lateral undulation closely resembles the simple undulatory motion observed in many other animals such as in lizards, eels and fish, in which waves of lateral bending propagate down the snakes body.

While the American Eel typically moves in an aquatic environment it can also move on land for short periods of time. It is able to successfully move about in both environments by producing traveling waves of lateral undulations. However, differences and terrestrial and aquatic locomotor strategy suggest that the axial musculature is being activated differently. In terrestrial locomotion, all points along the body move in the on approximately the same path and, therefore, the lateral displacements along the length of the eel's body is approximately the same. However, in aquatic locomotion, different points along the body follow different paths with increasing lateral amplitude more posteriorly. In general, the amplitude of the lateral undulation and angle of intervertebral flexion is much greater during terrestrial locomotion than that of aquatic.

A typical characteristic of many animals that utilize undulatory locomotion is that they have segmented muscles, or blocks of myomeres, running from their head to tails which are separated by connective tissue called myosepta. In addition, some segmented muscle groups, such as the of the lateral hypaxial musculature in the salamander are oriented at an angle to the longitudinal direction. For these obliquely oriented fiber the strain in the longitudinal direction is greater than the strain in the muscle fiber direction leading to an architectural gear ratio greater than 1. A higher initial angle of orientation and more dorsoventral bulging produces a faster muscle contraction but results in a lower amount of force production. It is hypothesized that animals employ a variable gearing mechanism that allows self-regulation of force and velocity to meet the mechanical demands of the contraction. When a pennate muscle is subjected to a low force, resistance to width changes in the muscle cause it to rotate which consequently produce a higher architectural gear ratio (AGR) (high velocity). However, when subject to a high force, the perpendicular fiber force component overcomes the resistance to width changes and the muscle compresses producing a lower AGR (capable of maintaining a higher force output).

Muscle Activity

In addition to a rostral to caudal kinematic wave that travels down the animals body during undulatory locomotion, there is also a corresponding wave of muscle activation that travels in the rostro-caudal direction. However, while this pattern is characteristic of undulatory locomotion, it too can vary with environment.

Aquatic Locomotion: Electromyogram (EMG) recordings reveal a similar pattern of muscle activation during aquatic movement as that of fish. At slow speeds only the most posterior end of the eels muscles are activated with more anterior muscle recruited at higher speeds As in many other animals, the muscles activate late in the lengthening phase of the muscle strain cycle, just prior to muscle shortening which is a pattern believed to maximize work output from the muscle.

Terrestrial Locomotion: EMG recording show a longer absolute duration and duty cycle of muscle activity during locomotion of land. Also, the absolute intensity is much higher while on land which is expect from the increase in gravitational forces acting on the animal. However, the intensity level decreases more posteriorly along the length of the eel's body. Also, the timing of muscle activation shifts to later in the strain cycle of muscle shortening.

Energetics

Animals with elongated bodies and reduced or no legs have evolved differently from their limbed relatives. In the past, some have speculated that this evolution was due to a lower energetic cost associated with limbless locomotion. The biomechanical arguments used to support this rational include that:

1. there is no cost associatied with the vertical displacement of the center of mass typically found with limbed animals;
2. there is no cost associated with accelerating or decelerating limbs; and
3. there is a lower cost for supporting the body.

This hypothesis has been studied further by examining the oxygen consumption rates in the snake during different modes of locomotion: lateral undulation, concertina and sidewinding. The *net cost of transport* (NCT), which indicates the amount of energy required to move a unit of mass a given distance, for a snake moving with a lateral undulatory gait is identical to that of a limbed lizard with the same mass.

However, a snake utilizing concertina locomotion produces a much higher net cost of transport, while sidewinding actually produces a lower net cost of transport. Therefore, the different modes of locomotion are of primary importance when determining energetic cost. The reason that lateral undulation has the same energetic efficiency as limbed animals and not less, as hypothesized earlier, might be due to the additional biomechanical cost associated with this type of movement due to the force needed to bend the body laterally, push its sides against a vertical surface, and overcome sliding friction.

Intersegmental Coordination

Wavelike motor pattern typically arise from a series of coupled segmental oscillator. Each segmental oscillator is capable of producing a rhythmic motor output in the absence of sensory feedback. One such example is the half center oscillator which consist of two neurons that are mutually inhibitory and produce activity 180° out of phase. The phase relationships between these oscillators are established by the emergent properties of the oscillators and the coupling between them. Forward swimming can by accomplished by a series of coupled oscillators in which the anterior oscillators have a shorter endogenous frequency than the posterior oscillators. In this case, all oscillators will be driven at the same period but the anterior oscillators will lead in phase. In addition, the phase relations can be established by asymmetries in the couplings between oscillators or by sensory feedback mechanisms.

Leech

The leech moves by producing dorsoventral undulations. The phase lags between body segments is about 20° and independent of cycle period. Thus, both hemisegments of the oscillator fire synchronously to produce a contraction. Only the ganglia rostral to the midpoint are capable of producing oscillation individually. There is U-shaped gradient in endogenous segment oscillation as well with the highest oscillations frequencies occurring near the middle of the animal. Although the couplings between neurons spans six segments in both the anterior and posterior direction, there are asymmetries between the various interconnections because the oscillators are active at three different phases. Those that are active in the 0° phase project only in the descending direction while those projecting in the ascending direction are active at 120° or 240°. In addition, sensory feedback from the environment may contribute to resultant phase lag.

Lamprey

The lamprey moves using lateral undulation and consequently left and right motor hemisegments are active 180° out of phase. Also, it has been found that the endogenous frequency of the more anterior oscillators is higher than that of the more posterior ganglia. In addition, inhibitory interneurons in the lamprey project 14-20 segments caudally but have short rostral projections. Sensory feedback may be important for appropriately responding to perturbations, but seems to be less important for maintaince of appropriate phase relations.

Based on biologically hypothesized connections of the central pattern generator in the salamander, a robotic system has been created which exhibits the same characteristics of the actual animal. Electrophysiology studies have shown that stimulation of the mesencephalic locomotor region (MLR) located in the brain of the salamander produce different gaits, swimming or walking, depending on intensity level. Similarly, the CPG model in the robot can exhibit walking at low levels of tonic drive and swimming at high levels of tonic drive. The model is based on the four assumptions that:

- Tonic stimulation of the body CPG produces spontaneous traveling waves. When the limb CPG is activated it overrides the body CPG.
- The strength of the coupling from the limb to the body CPG is stronger than that from body to limb.
- Limb oscillators saturate and stop oscillating at higher tonic drives.
- Limb oscillators have lower intrinsic frequencies than body CPGs at the same tonic drive.

This model encompasses the basic features of salamander locomotion.

Limbless Locomotion

There are a number of terrestrial and amphibious limbless vertebrates and invertebrates. These animals, due to lack of appendages, use their bodies to generate propulsive force. These movements are sometimes referred to as 'slithering' or 'crawling', although neither are formally used in the scientific literature and the latter term is also used for some animals moving on all four limbs. All limbless animals come from cold-blooded groups; there are no endothermic limbless animals, i.e. there are no limbless birds or mammals.

Lower Body Surface

Where the foot is important to the legged mammal, for limbless animals the underside of the body is important. Some animals such as snakes or legless lizards move on their smooth dry underside. Other animals have various features that aid movement. Molluscs such as slugs and snails move on a layer of mucus that is secreted from their underside, reducing friction and protecting from injury when moving over sharp objects. Earthworms have small bristles (setae) that hook into the substrate and help them move. Some animals such as leeches have suction cups on either end of the body allowing two anchor movement.

Type of Movement

Some limbless animals, such as leeches, have suction cups on either end of their body, which allow them to move by anchoring the rear end and then moving forward the front end, which is then anchored and then the back end is pulled in, and so on. This is known as two-anchor movement. A legged animal, the inchworm, also moves like this, clasping with appendages at either end of its body.

Limbless animals can also move using pedal locomotary waves, rippling the underside of the body. This is the main method used by molluscs such as slugs and snails, and also large flatworms, some other worms, and even earless seals.

The waves may move in the opposite direction to motion, known as retrograde waves, or in the same direction as motion, known as direct waves. Earthworms move by retrograde waves alternatively swelling and contracting down the length of their body, the swollen sections being held in place using setae. Aquatic molluscs such as limpets, which are sometimes out of the water, tend to move using retrograde waves. However terrestrial molluscs such as slugs and snails tend to use direct waves. Lugworms and seals also use direct waves.

Most snakes move using lateral undulation where a lateral wave travels down the snake's body in the opposite direction to the snake's motion and pushes the snake off irregularities in the ground. This mode of locomotion requires these irregularities to function. Another form of locomotion, rectilinear locomotion, is used at times by some snakes, especially large ones such as pythons and boa. Here large scales on the underside of the body, known as scutes are used to push backwards and downwards. This is effective on a flat surface and is used for slow, silent movement, such as when stalking prey. Snakes use concertina locomotion for moving slowly in tunnels, here the snake alternates in bracing parts of its body on it surrounds. Finally the caenophidian snakes use the fast and unusual method of movement known as sidewinding on sand or loose soil. The snake cycles through throwing the front part of its body in the direction of motion and bringing the back part of its body into line crosswise.

Rolling

Although animals have never evolved wheels for locomotion , a small number of animals will move at times by rolling their whole body. Rolling animals can be divided into those that roll under the force of gravity and those that roll using their own power.

Gravity Assisted

Web-toed salamander. This 10 cm long salamander lives on steep hills in the Sierra Nevada mountains. When it's disturbed or startled it coils itself up into a little ball often causing it to roll down hill.

Pebble toad (*Oreophrynella niger*). This toad lives atop tepui in the Guiana highlands of south america. When threatened, often by tarantulas, it rolls into ball, and typically being on an incline, rolls away under gravity like a loose pebble.

Namib wheeling spiders (*Carparachne spp.*), found in the Namib desert, will actively roll down sand dunes. This action can be used to successfully escape predators such as the *Pompilidae* tarantula wasps, which lays its eggs in a paralyzed spider so the larvae have enough food when they hatch. The spiders flip their body sideways and then cartwheel over their bent legs. The rotation is fast, with the golden wheel Spider (*Carparachne aureoflava*) moving up to 20 revolutions per second, moving the spider at one metre per second. At this speed the spider appears only as a blurred ball.

Pangolins, a type of mammal covered in thick scales rolls into a tight ball when threatened. Pangolins has been reported to roll away from danger, by both gravity and self-powered methods. A pangolin in hill country in Sumatra, to flee from the researcher, ran to the edge of a slope and curled into a ball to roll down the slope, crashing through the vegetation, and covering an estimated 30 metres or more in 10 seconds.

Self-powered

Caterpillar of the Mother-of-Pearl Moth, Pleuroptya ruralis. When attacked, this caterpillar will touch its head to its tail and roll backwards, up to 5 revolutions at about 40 cm per second, which is about 40 times its normal speed.

Nannosquilla decemspinosa, a species of long-bodied, short-legged Mantis Shrimp, lives in shallow sandy areas along the Pacific coast of Central and South America. When stranded by a low tide the 3 cm stomatopod lies on its back and performs backwards somersaults over and over. The animal moves up to 2 meters at a time by rolling 20-40 times, with speeds of around 72 revolutions per minute. That is 1.5 body lengths per second (3.5 cm/s). Researchers estimate that the stomatopod acts as a true wheel around 40 per cent of the time during this series of rolls. The remaining 60 per cent of the time it has to 'jumpstart' a roll by using its body to thrust itself upwards and forwards.

Pangolins have also been reported to roll away from danger by self-powered methods. Witnessed by a lion researcher in the Serengeti in Africa, a group of lions surrounded a pangolin, but could not get purchase on it when it rolled into a ball, and so the lions sat around it waiting and dozing. Surrounded by lions, it would unroll itself slightly and give itself a push to roll some distance, until by doing this multiple times it could get far enough away from the lions to be safe. Moving like this would allow a pangolin to cover distance while still remaining in a protective armoured ball.

Limits and Extremes

The fastest terrestrial animal is the cheetah, which can attain maximal sprint speeds of approximately 104 km/h (64 mph). The fastest running lizard is the Black Iguana, which has been recorded moving at speed of up to 34.9 km/h (21.7 mph).

6 Python Molurus

Python molurus is a large nonvenomous python species found in many tropic and subtropic areas of Southern and Southeast Asia. It is known by the common names Indian python, black-tailed python, and Indian rock python. Two subspecies are currently recognized: the nominate subspecies (*Python m. molurus*) and the Burmese Python (*Python m. bivittatus*). The nominate subspecies mainly described here is limited to Southern Asia, is generally lighter coloured than the Burmese Python and reaches usually 3 metres (9.8 ft).

Scientific Classification

Kingdom; Animalia Phylum; Chordata Subphylum; Vertebrata Class; Reptilia Order; Squamata Suborder; Serpentes Family; Pythonidae Genus; *Python* Species; *P. molurus*

Synonyms

[*Coluber*] *Molurus* - Linnaeus; 1758 *Boa Ordinata* - Schneider; 1801 *Boa Cinerae* - Schneider; 1801 *Boa Castanea* - Schneider; 1801 *Boa Albicans* - Schneider; 1801 *Boa Orbiculata* - Schneider; 1801 *Coluber Boaeformis* - Shaw; 1802 *Python bora* - Daudin; 1803 *Python tigris* - Daudin; 1803 *Python tigris castaneus* - Daudin; 1803 *Python tigris albanicus* - Daudin; 1803 *Python ordinatus* - Daudin; 1803 *Python Javanicus* - Kuhl; 1820 *Python molurus* - Gray; 1842 *Python Jamesonii* - Gray; 1842 *Python* (*Asterophis*) *tigris* - Fitzinger; 1843 *Python molurus* - Boulenger; 1893 *Python molurus* [*molurus*] - Werner; 1899 [*Python molurus*] var. *ocellatus* - Werner; 1899 [*Python molurus*] var. *intermedia* -

Werner; 1899 *Python molurus molurus* - Stull; 1935 *Python molurus* - M.A. Smith; 1943 *Python molurus pimbura* - Deraniyagala; 1945 *Python molurus molurus* - Stimson; 1969 [*Python molurus*] var. [*molurus*] - Deuve; 1970 *Python molurus* - Kluge, 1993.

The colour pattern is whitish or yellowish with the blotched patterns varying from shades of tan to dark brown. This varies with terrain and habitat. Specimens from the hill forests of Western Ghats and Assam are darker, while those from the Deccan Plateau and East Coast are usually lighter.

In Pakistan, Indian Pythons commonly reach a length of 2.4-3 metres (7.9-9.8 ft). In India, the nominate subspecies grows to 3 metres (9.8 ft) on average This value is supported by a 1990 study in Keoladeo National Park, where the biggest 25 per cent of the python population was 2.7-3.3 metres (8.9-11 ft) long. Only two specimen even measured nearly 3.6 metres (12 ft). Because of confusion with the Burmese Python, exaggerations and stretched skins in the past, the maximum length of this subspecies is hard to tell. The longest scientifically recorded specimen hailed from Pakistan and was 4.6 metres (15 ft) in length and weighing 52 kilograms . The nominate subspecies is found in Pakistan, India, Sri Lanka, southern Nepal, Bhutan, Bangladesh and probably in the north of Myanmar.

Habitat

Occurs in a wide range of habitats, including grasslands, swamps, marshes, rocky foothills, woodlands, "open" jungle and river valleys. They depend on a permanent source of water. Sometimes they can be found in abandoned mammal burrows, hollow trees, dense water reeds and mangrove thickets.

Behaviour

Lethargic and slow moving even in its native habitat, they exhibit little timidity and rarely try to escape even when attacked. Locomotion is usually rectilinear, with the body moving in a straight line. They are very good swimmers and are quite at home in water. They can be wholly submerged in water for many minutes if necessary, but usually prefer to remain near the bank.

These snakes feed on mammals, birds and reptiles indiscriminately, but seem to prefer mammals. Roused to activity on sighting prey, the snake will advance with quivering tail and lunge with open mouth. Live prey is constricted and killed. One or two coils are used to hold it in a tight grip. The prey, unable to breathe, succumbs and is subsequently swallowed head first. After a heavy meal, they are disinclined to move. If forced to, hard parts of the meal may tear through the body. Therefore, if disturbed, some specimens will disgorge their meal in order to escape from potential predators. After a heavy meal, an individual may fast for weeks, the longest recorded duration being 2 years. The python can swallow prey bigger than its diameter because the jaw bones are not connected. Morever prey cannot escape from its mouth because of the arrangement of the teeth (which are reverse saw-like). So far there have been no authentic cases of a human being eaten by this species.

Oviparous,up to 100 eggs are laid, protected and incubated by the female. Towards this end, it has been shown that they are capable of raising their body temperature above the ambient level through muscular contractions. The hatchlings are 45-60 cm (18-24 in) in length and grow quickly.

Conservation Status

These snakes have often been killed for their fine skin and are endangered. They are now partly protected by the Tamil Nadu Government. In Kerala and Tamil Nadu, the meat is eaten by locals as the fat is purported to have medicinal value. The Indian Python is classified as Lower Risk/Near Threatened on the IUCN Red List of Threatened Species (v2.3, 1996). This listing indicates that it may become threatened with extinction and is in need of frequent reassessment.

Pythonidae

The Pythonidae, commonly known simply as pythons, from the Greek word python- , are a family of non-venomous snakes found in Africa, Asia and Australia. Among its members are some of the largest snakes in the world. Eight genera and 26 species are currently recognized.

Found in subsaharan Africa, India, Myanmar, southern China, Southeast Asia and from the Philippines southeast through Indonesia to New Guinea and Australia.

In the United States an introduced population of Burmese pythons, *Python molurus bivittatus*, has existed as an invasive species in the Everglades National Park since the late 1990s.

Most members of this family are ambush predators, in that they typically remain motionless in a camouflaged position and then strike suddenly at passing prey. They will generally not attack humans unless startled or provoked, although females protecting their eggs can be aggressive. Large adult specimens can kill people. Unsuspecting children can and have been preyed upon and swallowed whole after being suffocated. Reports of attacks on human beings were once more common in South and Southeast Asia, but are now quite rare.

Prey is killed by a process known as *constriction;* after an animal has been grasped to restrain it, a number of coils are hastily wrapped around it. Then, by applying and maintaining sufficient pressure to prevent it from inhaling, the prey eventually succumbs due to asphyxiation. It has recently been suggested that the pressures produced during constriction cause cardiac arrest by interfering with blood flow, but this hypothesis has not yet been confirmed.

Larger specimens usually eat animals about the size of a house cat, but larger food items are known: some large Asian species have been known to take down adult deer, and the African rock python, *Python sebae*, has been known to eat antelope. Prey is swallowed whole, and may take anywhere from several days or even weeks to fully digest.

Contrary to popular belief, even the larger species, such as the reticulated python, *P. reticulatus*, do not crush their prey to death; in fact, prey is not even noticeably deformed before it is swallowed. The speed with which the coils are applied is impressive and the force they exert may be significant, but death is caused by suffocation, with the victim not being able to move its ribs to breathe while it is being constricted.

Pythonidae

The Pythonidae, commonly known simply as pythons, from the Greek word python- , are a family of non-venomous snakes found in Africa, Asia and Australia. Among its members are some of the largest snakes in the world. Eight genera and 26 species are currently recognized.

Found in subsaharan Africa, India, Myanmar, southern China, Southeast Asia and from the Philippines southeast through Indonesia to New Guinea and Australia.

In the United States an introduced population of Burmese pythons, *Python molurus bivittatus,* has existed as an invasive species in the Everglades National Park since the late 1990s.

Most members of this family are ambush predators, in that they typically remain motionless in a camouflaged position and then strike suddenly at passing prey. They will generally not attack humans unless startled or provoked, although females protecting their eggs can be aggressive. Large adult specimens can kill people. Unsuspecting children can and have been preyed upon and swallowed whole after being suffocated. Reports of attacks on human beings were once more common in South and Southeast Asia, but are now quite rare.

Prey is killed by a process known as *constriction;* after an animal has been grasped to restrain it, a number of coils are hastily wrapped around it. Then, by applying and maintaining sufficient pressure to prevent it from inhaling, the prey eventually succumbs due to asphyxiation. It has recently been suggested that the pressures produced during constriction cause cardiac arrest by interfering with blood flow, but this hypothesis has not yet been confirmed.

Larger specimens usually eat animals about the size of a house cat, but larger food items are known: some large Asian species have been known to take down adult deer, and the African rock python, *Python sebae,* has been known to eat antelope. Prey is swallowed whole, and may take anywhere from several days or even weeks to fully digest.

Contrary to popular belief, even the larger species, such as the reticulated python, *P. reticulatus,* do not crush their prey to death; in fact, prey is not even noticeably deformed before it is swallowed. The speed with which the coils are applied is impressive and the force they exert may be significant, but death is caused by suffocation, with the victim not being able to move its ribs to breathe while it is being constricted.

7 Anaconda

An anaconda is a large, non-venomous snake found in tropical South America. Although the name actually applies to a group of snakes, it is often used to refer only to one species in particular, the common or green anaconda, *Eunectes murinus*, which is one of the largest snakes in the world.

Anaconda may refer to:

- Any member of the genus *Eunectes*, a group of large, aquatic snakes found in South America.
- *Eunectes murinus*, a.k.a. the common anaconda, the largest species, found east of the Andes in Colombia, Venezuela, the Guianas, Ecuador, Peru, Bolivia, Brazil and on the island of Trinidad.
- *Eunectes notaeus*, a.k.a. the yellow anaconda, a smaller species found in eastern Bolivia, southern Brazil, Paraguay and northeastern Argentina.
- *Eunectes deschauenseei*, a.k.a. the dark-spotted anaconda, a rare species found in northeastern Brazil and coastal French Guiana.
- *E. beniensis*, a.k.a. the Bolivian anaconda, the most recently defined species found in the Departments of Beni and Pando in Bolivia.
- The giant anaconda, a mythical snake of enormous proportions found in South America.
- Any large snake that 'crushes' its prey. Applied loosely. Etymology.

The name was first used in the English language in 1768 by R. Edwin in a colourful description of a large snake found in Ceylon (now Sri Lanka), most likely a reticulated python, *Python reticulatus*. The account, which explains how the snake crushes and devours tigers, is full of popular misconceptions, but was much read at the time and so gave rise to the myth of the Anaconda of Ceylon.

Various theories exist regarding the origin of the name itself. One suggests that it was derived from the Sinhala *henakandaya*. However, this name is used to refer to the brown vine snake, *Ahaetulla pulverulenta*, a slender arboreal species that grows to five feet (152 cm) at most and feeds only on small vertebrates. Another theory by Yule and Burnell is based on an entry in the Catalogue of Indian Serpents from the Leyden Museum that reads: *Anacondaia Zeylonensibus, id est Bubalorum aliorumque jumentorum membra conterens*, meaning "the anacondaia of the Ceylonese, i.e. he that crushes the limbs of buffaloes and yoke beasts." Without a clear Sinhala connection, they suggest one from the Tamil language instead: *anai-kondra* (*anaik-konda*), meaning "which killed an elephant."

Giant Anaconda

Reports of giant anacondas date back as far as the discovery of South America when sightings of anacondas upwards of 50 meters (150 feet) began to circulate amongst colonists and the topic has been a subject of debate ever since among cryptozoologists and zoologists.

Anacondas normally grow to sizes of 6 metres (20 ft), and 250 kilograms (40 stone or approx, 550 lbs.) in weight. Although some python species can grow longer, the anaconda, particularly the Green Anaconda, is the heaviest and largest in terms of diameter of all snakes, and is often considered the biggest extant snake in the world. It is not uncommon for a fully grown anaconda to attack and kill a jaguar or caiman. The lengthiest reputably-measured and confirmed anacondas are about 7.5 meters (25 feet) long. Lengths of 50-60 feet have been reported for this species but such extremes lack verification and too add lack of large prey to support a super-large snake. The two only real reliable claims that can be found describe measured anacondas ranging from 26-34 feet although these remain unverified.

The first recorded sightings of giant anacondas were from the time of the discovery of South America, when early European explorers entered the dense jungles there and claimed to have seen giant snakes measuring up to 18 metres (59 ft) long. Natives also reported seeing anacondas upwards of 10.5 metres (34 ft) to 18 metres (59 ft). It is unquestionable that anacondas above 7 metres (23 ft) in length are rare; the Wildlife Conservation Society has, since the early 20th century, offered a large cash reward (worth US$60,000) for live delivery of any snake of 9 metres (30 ft) or more in length, but the prize has never been claimed despite the numerous sightings of giant anacondas. In a survey of 780 wild anacondas in Venezuela, the largest captured was 5 metres (16 ft) long, far short of the length required. A specimen measured in 1944 exceeded this size when a petroleum expedition in Colombia claimed to have measured an anaconda which was 11.4 metres (37 ft) in length, but its claim has never been proven. Scientist Vincent Roth also claimed to have shot and killed a 10.3 metres (34 ft) specimen, but like most other claims it lacks sound evidence. Another claim of an extraordinarily large anaconda was made by adventurer Percy Fawcett. During his 1906 expedition, Fawcett wrote that he had shot an anaconda that measured some 19 metres (62 ft) from nose to tail. Once published, Fawcett's account was widely ridiculed. Decades later, Belgian cryptozoologist Bernard Heuvelmans came to Fawcett's defence, arguing that Fawcett's writing was generally honest and reliable.

Historian Mike Dash writes of claims of still larger anacondas, alleged to be as long as 45 metres (148 ft), with some of the sightings supported with photos (although those photos lack scale). Dash notes that if reports of a 18 metres (59 ft) anaconda strains credulity, then a 120 feet (37 m) long specimen is generally regarded as an outright impossibility.

Perhaps the most well-known and defining portrayal of giant anaconda in popular fiction is the 1997 film *Anaconda,* which featured a giant anaconda hunting and killing several crew members from National Geographic, and its sequel *Anacondas: The Hunt for the Blood Orchid.* Another two sequels, *Anaconda 3: Offspring* and *Anacondas: Trail of Blood,* were produced as made-for-television movies in 2008.

Titanoboa

Titanoboa, pronounced , meaning "titanic boa," is a genus of snake that lived approximately 60 to 58 million years ago, in the Paleocene epoch, a 10-million-year period immediately following the dinosaur extinction event. The only known species is the *Titanoboa cerrejonensis,* the largest snake ever discovered, which supplanted the previous record holder, *Gigantophis.*

By comparing the sizes and shapes of its fossilized vertebrae to those of extant snakes, researchers estimated that the *T. cerrejonensis* reached a maximum length of 13 to 14 m (40 to 50 ft), weighed about 1,135 kg (2,500 lb), and measured about 1 m (3 ft) in diameter at the thickest part of the body.

The largest eight of the 28 *T. cerrejonensis* snakes found were between 13 and 14 m (40 and 50 ft) in length. In comparison, the largest extant snakes are the *Python reticulatus,* which measures up to 8.7 metres (29 ft) long, and the anaconda, which measures up to 5.21 metres (17 ft) long and is considered the heaviest snake on Earth. At the other end of the scale, the smallest extant snake is *Leptotyphlops carlae* with a length of about 10 centimetres (4 in).

In 2009, the fossils of 28 individual *T. cerrejonensis* were announced to have been found from the Cerrejón Formation in the coal mines of Cerrejón in La Guajira, Colombia. Prior to this discovery, few fossils of Paleocene-epoch vertebrates had been found in ancient tropical environments of South America. The snake was discovered on an expedition by a team of international scientists led by Jonathan Bloch, a

University of Florida vertebrate paleontologist, and Carlos Jaramillo, a paleobotanist from the Smithsonian Tropical Research Institute in Panama.

Because snakes are ectothermic, the discovery implies that the tropics, the creature's habitat, must have been warmer than previously thought, averaging approximately 30°C (90°F). The warmer climate of the Earth during the time of *T. cerrejonensis* allowed cold-blooded snakes to attain much larger sizes than modern snakes. Today, larger ectothermic animals are found in the tropics, where it is hottest, and smaller ones are found further from the equator.

It may well have been aquatic and hunted similar prey, like crocodiles. Indeed, other fossils from the Cerrejon pit include relatives of fishes, turtles and crocodiles - all suitable prey for Titanoboa. A 60-million-year-old relative of crocodiles described recently by University of Florida researchers in the Journal of Vertebrate Paleontology was likely a food source for Titanoboa, the largest snake the world has ever known.

8 Elapidae

Elapidae (Greek *éllops* = sea-fish) is a family of venomous snakes found in tropical and subtropical regions around the world, terrestrially in Asia, Australia, Africa, North America and South America and aquatically in the Pacific and Indian Oceans. Elapid snakes exist in a wide range of sizes, from 18 cm species of *Drysdalia* to the 5.6 m King Cobra, and are characterized by hollow, fixed fangs through which they inject venom. Currently, 61 genera that include 325 species are recognized.

All elapids have a pair of proteroglyphous fangs that are used to inject venom from glands located towards the rear of the upper jaws. In outward appearance terrestrial elapids look dissimilar to the Colubridae: almost all have long and slender bodies with smooth scales, a head that is covered with large shields and not always distinct from the neck, and eyes with round pupils. In addition, their behaviour is usually quite active and most are oviparous. There are exceptions to all these generalizations: e.g. the death adders (*Acanthophis*) include short and fat, rough-scaled, very broad-headed, cat-eyed, live-bearing, sluggish ambush predators with partly fragmented head shields.

Some elapids are strongly arboreal (African *Pseudohaje* and *Dendroaspis*, Australian *Hoplocephalus*), while many others are more or less specialised burrowers (e.g. *Ogmodon*, *Parapistocalamus*, *Simoselaps*, *Toxicocalamus*, *Vermicella*) in either humid or arid environments. Some species have very generalised diets, but many taxa have narrow prey preferences (stenophagy) and correlated morphological specialisations, e.g. for feeding on other snakes, elongate burrowing lizards, squamate eggs, mammals, birds, frogs, fish, etc.

Sea snakes (Hydrophiidae), which are also elapids, have adapted to a marine way of life in different ways and to various degrees. All have evolved paddle-like tails for swimming and the ability to excrete salt. Most also have laterally compressed bodies, ventral scales are much reduced in size, their nostrils are located dorsally (no internasal scales) and give birth to live young (ovoviviparous). In general, they have the ability to respire through their skin; experiments with the yellow-bellied sea snake, *Pelamis platurus*, have shown that this species can satisfy about 20 per cent of its oxygen requirements in this manner, allowing for prolonged dives. The sea kraits (*Laticauda* spp.), are the sea snakes least adapted to an aquatic life. They spend much of their time on land, where they lay their eggs. They have wide ventral scales, the tail is not as well-developed for swimming, and their nostrils are separated by internasal scales.

The fangs are the first two teeth on each maxillary bone, which are enlarged and hollow, and usually only one is in place on each side at any time. The maxilla is intermediate in length and mobility between typical colubrids (long, less mobile) and viperids (very short, highly mobile). When the mouth is closed, the fangs fit into grooved slots in the buccal floor; in the longest-fanged elapids (e.g. *Acanthophis, Oxyuranus*) it is common for the fangs to pierce right through the intermandibular skin, which does not seem to endanger the snake. The fangs are usually below the front edge of the eye and are angled backwards; due to this construction, most elapids must actually bite to envenomate. This action is therefore not as quick as with the viperids, that can envenomate with only a quick, stabbing motion. Some elapids (*Acanthophis, Oxyuranus, Dendroaspis, Ophiophagus*) have long fangs on quite mobile maxillae and can make first strike.

A few species are capable of spraying their venom from forward-facing holes at the tips of their fangs as a means of defense.

Geographic Range

On land, these snakes are found worldwide in tropical and subtropical regions, except in Europe. Sea snakes occur mainly in the Indian Ocean and the southwest Pacific. However, the range of one species, *Pelamis platura,* extends across the Pacific to the coasts of Central and South America.

Venom

All elapids are venomous and many are potentially deadly. The venoms are mostly neurotoxic which are considered more dangerous than the mainly proteolytic venoms of vipers. Many elapids are also large in size and can deliver a large quantity of highly potent venom; some examples are the Asiatic king cobra, the African black mamba, and the Australian Coastal taipan. Elapids use their venom both to immobilize their prey and in self defense.

In the past, many subfamilies were recognized, or have been suggested for the Elapidae, including the Elapinae, Hydrophiinae, Micrurinae (coral snakes), Acanthophiinae (Australian elapids) and the Laticaudinae (sea kraits). Currently, none are universally recognized. There is now good molecular evidence via karyotyping and protein electrophoretic analysis, immunological distance, DNA sequence analysis etc for reciprocal monophyly of two groups: the African, Asian and New World Elapinae, and Australasian and marine Hydrophiinae. Thus, the Australian terrestrial elapids are 'hydrophiines', though not sea snakes, while it is believed that Laticauda and the 'true sea snakes' evolved separately from among the Australasian land-snakes. Asian cobras, coral snakes, and American coral snakes also appear to be monophyletic, while African cobras do not.

The type genus for the Elapidae was originally *Elaps,* but that group was moved to another family. In contrast to what usually happens in botany, the *Elapidae* family was not renamed. In the meantime, *Elaps* was renamed *Homoroselaps* and moved back to the *Elapidae*. However, it as a sister taxon to *Atractaspis* which should therefore have been assigned to the *Atractaspididae*.

Cobra

Cobra is a venomous snake belonging to the family Elapidae. However, not all snakes commonly referred to as cobras are of the same genus, or even of the same family. The name is short for *cobra de capelo* or *cobra-de-capelo*, which is Portuguese for 'snake with hood', or 'hood-snake'. When disturbed, most of these snakes can rear up and spread their neck (or hood) in a characteristic threat display.

Cobra may refer to:

- any member of the genus *Naja*, also known as typical cobras (with the characteristic ability to raise the front quarters of their bodies off the ground and flatten their necks in a threatening gesture), a group of venomous elapids found in Africa and Asia;
- spitting cobras, a subset of *Naja* species with the ability to eject venom from its fangs in self-defense;
- any member of the genus *Boulengerina*, a.k.a. water cobras, a group of venomous elapids found in Africa;
- any member of the genus *Aspidelaps*, a.k.a. shield-nose cobras or coral snakes, a group of venomous elapids found in Africa;
- any member of the genus *Pseudohaje*, a.k.a. tree cobras, a group of venomous elapids found in Africa;
- *Paranaja multifasciata*, a.k.a. the burrowing cobra, a venomous elapid species found in Africa;
- *Ophiophagus hannah*, a.k.a. the king cobra, a venomous elapid species found in India and southern Asia;
- *Hemachatus haemachatus*, a.k.a. the ringhals or ring-necked spitting cobra, a venomous elapid species found in Africa;
- *Micrurus fulvius*, a.k.a. the American cobra or eastern coral snake, a venomous elapid species found in the southeastern United States;

- *Hydrodynastes gigas*, a.k.a. the false water cobra, a mildly venomous colubrid species found in South America;
- a taxonomic synonym for the genus *Bitis*, a.k.a. puff adders, a group of venomous vipers found in Africa and in the south of the Arabian Peninsula.

King Cobra

The king cobra (*Ophiophagus hannah*) is the world's longest venomous snake, with a length up to 5.6 m (18.5 ft). This species is widespread throughout Southeast Asia and parts of India, and is found mostly in forested areas. The king cobra can be fierce and agile, and can deliver a large quantity of highly potent venom in a single bite. It is one of the most dangerous and feared Asiatic snakes.

The King Cobra is a large and powerful snake, averaging 3.6-4 m (12-13 feet) in length and typically weighing about 6 kg (13.2 lb). A particularly large specimen was kept captive at the London Zoo, and grew to 5.7 m (18.8 ft) before being euthanized upon the outbreak of World War II. Despite their large size, king cobras are fast and agile.

The skin of this snake is either olive-green, tan, or black, and it has faint, pale yellow cross bands down the length of the body. The belly is cream or pale yellow, and the scales are smooth. Juveniles are shiny black with narrow yellow bands (can be mistaken for a banded krait, but readily identified with its expanded hood). The head of a mature snake can be quite massive and bulky in appearance, though like all snakes, they can expand their jaws to swallow large prey items. It has proteroglyph dentition, meaning it has two short, fixed fangs in the front of the mouth which channel venom into the prey like hypodermic needles. The male is larger and thicker than the female. The average lifespan of a king cobra is about 20 years.

Identification

The king cobra is the sole member of genus Ophiophagus, while most other cobras are members of the genus Naja. They can be distinguished from other cobras by size and hood marks. King cobras are larger than other cobras, and the stripe on the neck is like the symbol '^' instead of a double or single eye(s) shape that may be seen in most of the other cobras. A foolproof method of identification if the head is clearly visible is the presence of a pair of large scales known as occipitals, at the back of the top of the head. These are behind the usual 'nine-plate' arrangement typical of colubrids and elapids, and are unique to the king cobra.

Scalation

Dorsal scales: midbody 15 rows; *Ventral scales:* Males 235-250, females 239-265; *Tail:* Subcaudal scales single or paired in each row, 83-96 in males and 77-98 in females.

The king cobra is distributed across South Asia, Southeast Asia, and the southern areas of East Asia (southern China) but is not common. It lives in dense highland forests, preferring areas dotted with lakes and streams. King cobra populations have dropped in some areas of its range because of the destruction of forests, but despite this, the snake is not listed by the IUCN as in danger of becoming extinct.

Behaviour

King cobras, like other snakes, receive chemical information ('smell') via their forked tongues, which pick up scent particles and transfer them to a special sensory receptor (Jacobson's organ) located in the roof of its mouth. When the scent of a meal is detected, the snake flicks its tongue to gauge the prey's location (the twin forks of the tongue acting in stereo); it also uses its keen eyesight (king cobras are able to detect moving prey almost 100 m [300 feet] away), intelligence and sensitivity to earth-borne vibration to track its prey. Following envenomation, the king cobra will begin to swallow its struggling prey while its toxins begin the digestion of its victim. King cobras, like all snakes, have flexible jaws. The jaw bones are connected by pliable ligaments, enabling the lower jaw bones to move independently, enabling the King cobra to swallow its prey whole. The expansion of the jaw enables the snake to swallow prey much larger than its head.

King cobras are able to hunt at all times of day, although it is rarely seen at night, leading most herpetologists to classify it as a diurnal species.

The king cobra can be highly aggressive. When threatened, it raises up the anterior portion of its body, flattening the neck, showing the fangs and hissing loudly. (Bioacoustic analysis of the 'growl' of the king cobra has shown that it differs significantly from other snakes. Generally a typical snake hiss has a broad-frequency span (~3,000 to 13,000 Hz) with a dominant frequency near 7,500 Hz, whereas the 'growl' of the king cobra consists of frequencies below 2,500 Hz, with a dominant frequency near 600 Hz.) It is easily irritated by closely approaching objects or sudden movements. The king cobra attacks quickly, and the strike distance is about 2 m (7 feet); people can easily misjudge the safe distance. The king cobra may deliver multiple bites in a single attack, or bite and hold on. Although it is a highly dangerous snake, it prefers to escape unless it is cornered or provoked.

If a king cobra encounters a natural predator, such as the mongoose, which has some resistance to the neurotoxins, the snake generally tries to flee. If unable to do so, it forms the distinctive cobra hood and emits a hiss, sometimes with feigned closed-mouth strikes. These efforts usually prove to be very effective, especially since it is more dangerous than other mongoose prey, as well as being much too large for the small mammal to kill with ease.

Diet

The king cobra's genus name, Ophiophagus, means 'snake-eater', and its diet consists primarily of other snakes, including ratsnakes, sizeable pythons and even other venomous snakes (including kraits, cobras and smaller members of its own species). When food is scarce, they may also feed on other small vertebrates, such as lizards, birds, and rodents. In some cases, the cobra may 'constrict' its prey, such as birds and larger rodents, using its muscular body, though this is uncommon. After a large meal, the snake may live for many months without another one because of its slow metabolic rate. The king cobra's most common meal is the ratsnake; pursuit of this species often brings king cobras close to human settlements.

The venom of the king cobra consists primarily of neurotoxins, but it also contains cardiotoxic compounds. Toxic constituents are mainly proteins and polypeptides.

During a bite, venom is forced through the snake's half-inch (1.25 cm) fangs into the wound, and quickly attacks the victim's central nervous system, inducing severe pain, blurred vision, vertigo, drowsiness, and paralysis. Envenomation progresses to cardiovascular collapse, and the victim falls into a coma. Death soon follows due to respiratory failure.

In the past, the LD_{50} of the king cobra's venom was treated as 1.6 mg/kg - 1.8 mg/kg (which was one of the least venomous elapids). However, in recent toxicology study the LD_{50} of Chinese king cobra venom was found to be 0.34 mg/kg . The value is lower than that of many Naja species found in the same habitats (such as the Chinese cobra), showing that the king cobra can actually be more venomous than many other cobras. The king cobra is also capable of delivering larger quantities of venom than most other snakes, injecting a 380-600 mg dose in a single bite on average. It was reported that a single bite from this species can kill an adult Asian elephant. A bite from the king cobra can cause the death of a healthy adult human within 15 minutes, though the average death time recorded is between 30-45 minutes after envenomation. The mortality rate from a bite can be over 75 per cent, depending upon treatment details. It is regarded as one of the deadliest snakes in the world.

There are two types of antivenom made specifically to treat king cobra envenomations. The Red Cross in Thailand manufactures one, and the Central Research Institute in India manufactures the other; however, both are made in small quantities and are not widely available. Ohanin, a protein component of the venom, causes hypolocomotion and hyperalgesia in mammals. Other components have cardiotoxic, cytotoxic and neurotoxic effects. In Thailand, a concoction of alcohol and the ground root of turmeric is ingested, which has been clinically shown to create a strong resilience against the venom of the king cobra, and other snakes with neurotoxic venom.

The king cobra is unique among snakes in that the female king cobra is a very dedicated parent. She makes a nest for her eggs, scraping up leaves and other debris into a mound in which to deposit them, and remains in the nest until the young hatch.

A female usually deposits 20 to 40 eggs into the mound, which acts as an incubator. She stays with the eggs and guards the mound tenaciously, rearing up into a threat display if any large animal gets too close.

Inside the mound the eggs are incubated at a steady 28°C (82°F). When the eggs start to hatch, instinct causes the female to leave the nest and find prey to eat so she does not eat her young. The baby king cobras have a length of 45 to 55 centimeters (18 to 22 in). They are highly aggressive, and their venom is as deadly as that of an adult.

Bungarus

Bungarus, commonly referred to as kraits (pronounced krits), is a genus of venomous elapid snakes found in South and South-East Asia. There are 12 species and five subspecies recognized.

Kraits usually range between 1 and 1.5 m in length, although specimens as large as two m have been observed. The Banded Krait (*B. fasciatus*) may grow as large as 2.5 m. Most species of krait are covered in smooth glossy scales that are arranged in bold striped patterns of alternating black and light-coloured areas. This gives the snake camouflage in its habitat of grassland and scrub jungle. The scales along the dorsal ridge of the back are hexagonal. The head is slender and the eyes have round pupils. Kraits have a pronounced dorsolateral flattening, and are triangular in cross section. The tail tapers to a thin point.

Diet and Behaviour

Kraits are ophiophagous, preying primarily upon other snakes (including venomous varieties) and are cannibalistic, feeding on other kraits. They will also eat mice and small lizards.

All kraits are nocturnal. They are more docile during the daylight hours; at night they become very active, but are not very aggressive even when provoked. They are actually rather timid, and will often hide their heads within their coiled bodies for protection. When in this posture, they will sometimes whip their tail around as a type of distraction.

Bungarus species have highly potent neurotoxic venom which can induce muscle paralysis. Clinically, their venom contains mostly pre-synaptic neurotoxins. These affect the ability of neuron endings to properly release the chemical that sends the message to the next neuron. Following envenomation with bungarotoxins, transmitter release is initially blocked (leading to a brief paralysis), followed by a period of massive overexcitation (cramps, tremors, spasms), which finally tails off to paralysis. These phases may not be seen in all parts of the body at the same time. Since kraits are nocturnal they seldom encounter humans during daylight hours, so bites are rare and they may prefer to deliver non-fatal bites, but a bite from a krait is potentially life-threatening, and should be regarded as a medical emergency.

Typically, victims start to complain later of severe abdominal cramps accompanied by progressive muscular paralysis, frequently starting with ptosis. As there are no local symptoms, a patient should be carefully observed for tell-tale signs of paralysis (e.g. the onset of ptosis, diplopia and dysphagia) and treated urgently with antivenom. Prior to the availability of the antivenom,the mortality rate among the victims bitten can be high (the rate is various among different species). There is frequently little or no pain at the site of a krait bite, which can provide false reassurance to the victim. Several websites state the statement that there is a mortality rate of 50 per cent even with treatment, but there is no original source in the medical literature for this statement. The major medical difficulty of patients envenomated are the lack of medical resources (especially intubation supplies and mechanical ventilators in rural hospitals) and the ineffectiveness of the antivenom. Definitive care may also be delayed as patients may first visit the local *mantrik* or *tantrik*, a holy person and traditional healer who may attempt to rid the body of the venom with spells or herbal remedies, which are ineffective interventions.

Once at a healthcare facility support must be provided until the venom is metabolised and the victim can breathe unaided, especially if there is no species-specific antivenom available. Given that the toxins alter acetylcholine transmission which causes the paralysis, some patients have been successfully treated with cholinesterase inhibitors such as physostigmine or neostigmine, but success is variable and may be species dependent as well. If death occurs it typically takes place approximately 6 to 12 hours after the krait bite, but can be significantly delayed. Cause of death is usually respiratory failure i.e. suffocation via complete paralysis of the diaphragm. Even if patients make it to a hospital subsequent permanent coma and even brain death from hypoxia may occur given potentially long transport times to get medical care.

The polyvalent Elapid Antivenom is effective in neutralizing of the venoms of *Bungarus candidus* and *Bungarus flaviceps* and rather effective in the neutralization of the venom of *Bungarus fasciatus*. In this last case, the monovalent *Bungarus fasciatus* antivenom is also moderately effective.

Coral Snake

The coral snakes are a large group of elapid snakes that can be subdivided into two distinct groups, Old World coral snakes and New World coral snakes. There are 11 species of Old World coral snake in one genus (*Calliophis*), and over 65 recognized species of New World coral snakes in three genera (*Leptomicrurus*, *Micruroides*, and *Micrurus*).

Coral snakes are most notable for their red, yellow/white, and black coloured banding. (However, several nonvenomous species have similar colouration, including the scarlet snake, genus *Cemophora*, some of the kingsnakes and milk snakes, genus Lampropeltis, and the shovelnose snakes, genus *Chionactis*.) In some regions, the order of the bands distinguishes between the non-venomous mimics and the venomous coral snakes, inspiring some folk rhymes— "Red on yellow, kill a fellow; "Red on black, friend of Jack"; and "Red into black, venom lack; red into yellow, kill a fellow." However, this reliably applies only to coral snakes native to North America: *Micrurus fulvius* (Eastern or common coral snake), *Micrurus tener* (Texas coral snake), and *Micruroides euryxanthus* (Arizona coral snake), found in the southern and western United States. Coral snakes found in other parts of the world can have distinctly different patterns, have red bands touching black bands, have only pink and blue banding, or have no banding at all.

Most species of coral snake are small in size. North American species average around 3 feet (91 cm) in length, but specimens of up to 5 feet (150 cm) or slightly larger have been reported. Aquatic species have flattened tails acting as a fin, aiding in swimming.

Coral snakes vary widely in their behaviour, but most are very elusive, fossorial snakes which spend the vast majority of their time buried beneath the ground or in the leaf litter of a rainforest floor, only coming to the surface while raining or during breeding season. Some species, like *Micrurus surinamensis* are almost entirely aquatic and spend most of their lives in slow-moving bodies of water that have dense vegetation.

Like all elapid snakes, coral snakes use a pair of small fangs fixed in the front of their top jaw to deliver their venom. They feed on smaller snakes, lizards, frogs, and nestling birds and rodents etc. The venom takes time to fully take effect.

Coral snakes have a tendency to hold on to a victim when biting, unlike vipers which have retractable fangs and tend to prefer to strike and let go immediately. Coral snakes are not aggressive or prone to biting however, and account for less than one percent of the number of snake bites each year in the United States. Most coral snake bites in the United States are legitimate occurring because of accidental contact with the snake while engaged in an outdoor activity such as gardening.

New World coral snakes exist in the southern range of many temperate U.S. states.

Coral Snakes are found in scattered localities in the southern Coastal Plain from North Carolina to Louisiana, including all of Florida. They can be found in pine and scrub oak sandhills habitats in parts of this range but sometimes inhabit hardwood areas and pine flatwoods that undergo seasonal flooding.

There is controversy about the classification of the very similar Texas coral snake as a separate species. Its habitat, in Texas, Louisiana, and Arkansas, is separated from the eastern habitat by the Mississippi River. The map here shows the denser population in the southeast United States but coral snakes have been spotted as far north as Kentucky.

The Arizona coral snake, clearly a separate species and genus, is found in central and southern Arizona, extreme southwestern New Mexico and southward to Sinaloa in western Mexico. It occupies arid and semiarid regions in many different habitat types including thornscrub, desert-scrub, woodland, grassland and farmland. It is found in the plains and lower mountain slopes from sea level to 5800 feet (1768 m); often found in rocky areas.

New World coral snakes possess one of the most potent venoms of any North American snake. Most venomous snakes must inject between 75-100 mg of venom to be fatal. However, relatively few bites are recorded due to their reclusive nature and the fact they generally inhabit sparsely populated areas. According to the American National Institutes of Health, there are an average of 15-25 coral snake bites in the United States each year.

When confronted by humans, coral snakes will almost always attempt to flee, and bite only as a last resort. In addition, coral snakes have short fangs (proteroglyph dentition) that cannot penetrate thick leather clothing. Any skin penetration however, is a medical emergency that requires immediate attention. Coral snakes have a powerful neurotoxin that paralyzes the breathing muscles; mechanical or artificial respiration, along with large doses of antivenin, are often required to save a victim's life. There is usually only mild pain associated with a bite, but respiratory failure can occur within hours.

The bite of a coral snake may soon become increasingly more dangerous, ironically because of the relatively few bites each year. Production of coral snake antivenin in the United States has ceased because it is not profitable. According to Pfizer, the owner of the company that used to make Coralmyn, it would take over $5–$10 million to put toward researching a new synthetic antivenom. The cost was just too large for the small number of cases presented each year. The current antivenin stock expired in 2010, after two consecutive expiration date extensions approved by the FDA. Foreign pharmaceutical manufacturers have produced other coral snake antivenins, but the costs associated with licensing them in the United States have stalled availability .

Taxonomy

Animalia, Deuterostomia, Chordata - Vertebrata - Gnathostomata, Reptilia, Squamata, Serpentes, Elapidae.

Old World

Genus *Calliophis* Wikispecies has information related to *Calliophis*.

New World

Genus *Leptomicrurus*

Guyana Blackback Coral Snake *Leptomicrurus collaris* - northern South America.

Leptomicrurus collaris collaris (Schlegel, 1837)

Leptomicrurus collaris breviventris *(Roze & Bernal-Carlo, 1987)*

Andes/Andean Blackback Coral Snake, *Leptomicrurus narduccii*

Leptomicrurus narduccii narduccii (Jan, 1863)

Leptomicrurus narduccii melanotus (Peters, 1881)

Arizona Coral Snake, *Micruroides euryxanthus* - lowland regions from Arizona to Sinaloa.

Micruroides euryxanthus australis (Zweifel & Norris, 1955)

Micruroides euryxanthus euryxanthus (Kennicott, 1860)

Micruroides euryxanthus neglectus (Roze, 1967)

Genus *Micrurus*

Allen's Coral Snake, *Micrurus alleni* - eastern Nicaragua, Costa Rica, and Panama.

Micrurus alleni alleni (Schmidt, 1936)

Micrurus alleni richardi (Taylor, 1951)

Micrurus alleni yatesi (Taylor, 1954)

Micrurus altirostris (Cope, 1860) - Brazil, Uruguay, and northeastern Argentina.

Regal Coral Snake, *Micrurus ancoralis* - southeastern Panama, western Colombia, and western Ecuador

Micrurus ancoralis jani (Schmidt, 1936)

Micrurus ancoralis ancoralis (Jan, 1872)

Annellated Coral Snake, *Micrurus annellatus* - southeastern Ecuador, eastern Peru, Bolivia, and western Brazil.

Micrurus annellatus annellatus (Peters, 1871)

Micrurus annellatus balzanii (Boulenger, 1898)

Micrurus annellatus bolivianus (Roze, 1967)

Black-headed Coral Snake, *Micrurus averyi* (Schmidt, 1939)

Micrurus bernadi (Cope, 1887) - Mexico.

Ecuadorian Coral Snake, *Micrurus bocourti* (Jan, 1872) - western Ecuador to northern Colombia.

Bogert's Coral Snake, *Micrurus bogerti* (Roze, 1967) - Oaxaca.

Brown's Coral Snake, *Micrurus browni* - Quintana Roo to Honduras.

Micrurus browni browni (Schmidt & Smith, 1943)
Micrurus browni importunus (Roze, 1967)
Micrurus browni Taylori (Schmidt & Smith, 1943)
Micrurus camilae (Renjifo & Lundberg, 2003) - Colombia
Catamayo Coral Snake, *Micrurus catamayensis* (Roze, 1989) - Catamayo Valley of Ecuador
Clark's Coral Snake, *Micrurus clarki* (Schmidt, 1936) - southeastern Costa Rica to western Colombia
Painted Coral Snake, *Micrurus corallinus* (Merrem, 1820)
Brazilian Coral Snake, *Micrurus decoratus* (Jan, 1858)
Micrurus diana (Roze, 1983)
Variable Coral Snake, *Micrurus diastema*
Micrurus diastema diastema (Duméril, Bibron, & Duméril, 1854)
Micrurus diastema aglaeope (Cope, 1859)
Micrurus diastema alienus (Werner, 1903)
Micrurus diastema affinis (Jan, 1858)
Micrurus diastema apiatus (Jan, 1858)
Micrurus diastema macdougalli (Roze, 1967)
Micrurus diastema sapperi (Werner, 1903)
Pygmy Coral Snake, *Micrurus dissoleucus*
Micrurus dissoleucus dissoleucus (Cope, 1860)
Micrurus dissoleucus dunni (Barbour, 1923)
Micrurus dissoleucus melanogenys (Cope, 1860)
Micrurus dissoleucus meridensis (Roze, 1989)
Micrurus dissoleucus nigrirostris (Schmidt, 1955)
West Mexican Coral Snake, *Micrurus distans*
Micrurus distans distans (Kennicott, 1860)
Micrurus distans michoacanensis (Duges, 1891)
Micrurus distans oliveri (Roze, 1967)
Micrurus distans zweifeli (Roze, 1967)
Micrurus dumerilii
Micrurus dumerili antioquiensis (Schmidt, 1936)

Micrurus dumerili carinicaudus (Schmidt, 1936)
Micrurus carinicauda (Schmidt, 1936)
Micrurus dumerili colombianus (Griffin, 1916)
Micrurus dumerili transandinus (Schmidt, 1936)
Micrurus dumerili venezuelensis (Roze, 1989)
Elegant Coral Snake, *Micrurus elegans*
Micrurus elegans elegans (Jan, 1858)
Micrurus elegans veraepacis (Schmidt, 1933)
Oaxacan Coral Snake, *Micrurus ephippifer*
Micrurus ephippifer zapotecus (Roze, 1989)
Micrurus ephippifer ephippifer (Cope, 1886)
Slender Coral Snake, *Micrurus filiformis*
Micrurus filiformis filiformis (Günther, 1859)
Micrurus filiformis subtilis (Roze, 1967)
Southern Coral Snake, *Micrurus frontalis* - Brazil to northeastern Argentina
Micrurus frontalis frontalis (Duméril, Bibron, & Duméril, 1854)
Micrurus frontalis brasiliensis (Roze, 1967)
Micrurus frontalis mesopotamicus (Barrio & Miranda 1967)
Bolivian Coral Snake, *Micrurus frontifasciatus* (Werner, 1927)
Eastern Coral Snake, *Micrurus fulvius* (Linnaeus, 1766) - coastal plains of North Carolina to Louisiana
Hemprich's Coral Snake, *Micrurus hemprichii*
Micrurus hemprichii hemprichii (Jan, 1858)
Micrurus hemprichii ortoni (Schmidt, 1953)
Micrurus hemprichii rondonianus (Roze & Da Silva [*disambiguation needed*], 1990)
Mayan Coral Snake, *Micrurus hippocrepis* (Peters, 1862)
Caatinga Coral Snake, *Micrurus ibiboboca* (Merrem, 1820)
Venezuela Coral Snake, *Micrurus isozonus* (Cope, 1860)
Langsdorff's Coral Snake, *Micrurus langsdorffi*
Micrurus langsdorffi langsdorffi (Wagler, 1824)

Micrurus langsdorffi ornatissimus (Jan, 1858)
Balsan Coral Snake, *Micrurus laticollaris*
Micrurus laticollaris laticollaris (Peters, 1870)
Micrurus laticollaris maculirostris (Roze, 1967)
Broad-ringed Coral Snake, *Micrurus latifasciatus* (Schmidt, 1933)
South American Coral Snake, *kayla lemniscatus* - most of low lying areas of South America.
Micrurus lemniscatus lemniscatus (Linnaeus, 1758)
Micrurus lemniscatus carvalhoi (Roze, 1967)
Micrurus lemniscatus diutius (Burger, 1955)
Micrurus lemniscatus frontifasciatus (Werner, 1927)
Micrurus lemniscatus helleri (Schmidt & Schmidt, 1925)
Tuxtlan Coral Snake, *Micrurus limbatus*
Micrurus limbatus limbatus (Fraser, 1964)
Micrurus limbatus spilosomus (Perez-Higaredo & Smith, 1990)
Speckled Coral Snake, *Micrurus margaritiferus* (Roze, 1967)
Micrurus medemi (Roze, 1967)
Mertens' Coral Snake, *Micrurus mertensi* (Schmidt, 1936)
Redtail Coral Snake *Micrurus mipartitus*
Micrurus mipartitus mipartitus (Duméril, Bibron, & Duméril, 1854)
Micrurus mipartitus anomalus (Boulenger, 1896)
Micrurus mipartitus decussatus (Duméril, Bibron, & Duméril, 1854)
Micrurus mipartitus semipartitus (Jan, 1858)
Many-banded Coral Snake, *Micrurus multifasciatus*
Micrurus multifasciatus multifasciatus (Jan, 1858)
Micrurus multifasciatus hertwigi (Werner, 1897)
Cauca Coral Snake, *Micrurus multiscutatus* (Rendahl & Vestergren, 1940)
Cloud Forest Coral Snake, *Micrurus nebularis* (Roze, 1989)

Central American Coral Snake, *Micrurus nigrocinctus* - Yucatan and Chiapas to Colombia as well as western Caribbean islands
Micrurus nigrocinctus babaspul (Roze, 1967)
Micrurus nigrocinctus coibensis (Schmidt, 1936)
Micrurus nigrocinctus divaricatus (Hallowell, 1855)
Micrurus nigrocinctus mosquitensis (Schmidt, 1933)
Micrurus nigrocinctus nigrocinctus (Girard, 1854)
Micrurus nigrocinctus ovandoensis (Schmidt & Smith, 1943)
Micrurus nigrocinctus wagneri (Mertens, 1941)
Micrurus nigrocinctus yatesi (Dunn, 1942)
Micrurus nigrocinctus zunilensis (Schmidt, 1932)
Micrurus pacaraimae (Morata de Carvalho, 2002)
Micrurus pachecogili (Campbell, 2000)
Micrurus paraensis (Da Cunha & Nascimento, 1973)
Peruvian Coral Snake, *Micrurus peruvianus* (Schmidt, 1936)
Peters' Coral Snake, *Micrurus petersi* (Roze, 1967)
Nayarit Coral Snake, *Micrurus proximans* (Smith & Chrapliwy, 1958)
Carib Coral Snake, *Micrurus psyches*
Micrurus psyches circinalis (Duméril, Bibron & Duméril, 1854)
Micrurus psyches donosoi (Hoge, Cordeiro, & Romano, 1976)
Micrurus psyches psyches (Daudin, 1803)
Putumayo Coral Snake, *Micrurus putumayensis* (Lancini, 1962)
Micrurus pyrrhocryptus (Cope, 1862)
Micrurus remotus (Roze, 1987)
Micrurus renjifoi (Lamar, 2003)
Roatan Coral Snake, *Micrurus ruatanus* (Günther, 1895)
Santander Coral Snake, *Micrurus sangilensis* (Nicéforo-Maria, 1942)
Micrurus scutiventris (Hoge, & Romano-Hoge, 1966)

Micrurus silviae Di-Bernardo et al., 2007
Amazon Coral Snake, *Micrurus spixii*
Micrurus spixii spixii (Wagler, 1824)
Micrurus spixiii martiusi (Schmidt, 1953)
Micrurus spixii obscurus (Jan, 1872)
Micrurus spixii princeps (Boulenger, 1905)
Micrurus spurelli (Boulenger, 1914)
Steindachner's Coral Snake, *Micrurus steindachneri*
Micrurus steindachneri steindachneri (Werner, 1901)
Micrurus steindachneri orcesi (Roze, 1967)
Panamanian Coral Snake, *Micrurus stewarti* (Barbour & Amaral, 1928)
Stuart's Coral Snake, *Micrurus stuarti* (Roze, 1967)
Aquatic Coral Snake, *Micrurus surinamensis*
Micrurus surinamensis surinamensis (Cuvier, 1817)
Micrurus surinamensis nattereri (Schmidt, 1952)
Micrurus tamaulipensis (Lavin-Murcio & Dixon, 2004) - Sierra Madre Oriental in Tamaulipas.
Texas Coral Snake, *Micrurus tener* - Texas and Louisiana south to Morelos and Guanajuato.
Micrurus tener fitzingeri (Jan, 1858)
Micrurus tener maculatus (Roze, 1967)
Micrurus tener microgalbineus (Brown, & Smith, 1942)
Micrurus tener tener (Baird, & Girard, 1853)
Micrurus tricolour (Hoge, 1956)
Desert Coral Snake, *Micrurus tschudii* (Jan, 1858)
Micrurus tschudii olssoni (Schmidt & Schmidt, 1925)
Micrurus tschudii tschudii (Jan, 1858)

New World coral snakes serve as models for their Batesian mimics, False coral snakes, snake species whose venom is less toxic, as well as for many nonvenomous snake species that bear superficial resemblances to them. The role of coral snakes as models for Batesian mimics is supported by research showing that coral snake colour patterns deter predators from attacking snake-shaped prey, and that in the absence of coral snakes, species hypothesized to mimic them are indeed attacked more frequently. Species that appear similar to coral snakes include:

- *Erythrolamprus aesculapii*
- *Erythrolamprus bizona*
- *Erythrolamprus ocellatus* (AKA Tobago False Coral)
- *Oxyrhopus petola*
- *Lampropeltis pyromelana*
- *Chionactis palarostris*
- Milk snake (*Lampropeltis triangulum*) subspecies
- *Lampropeltis triangulum multistrata*
- *Lampropeltis triangulum elapsoides*
- *Lampropeltis triangulum amaura*
- *Lampropeltis triangulum gentilis*
- *Lampropeltis triangulum annulata*
- *Lampropeltis zonata*
- *Cemophora coccinea*

9 Viperidae

The Viperidae are a family of venomous snakes found all over the world, except in Antarctica, Australia, Ireland, New Zealand, Madagascar, Hawaii, various other isolated islands and above the Arctic Circle. All have relatively long, hinged fangs that permit deep penetration and injection of venom. Four subfamilies are currently recognized.

All viperids have a pair of relatively long solenoglyphous (hollow) fangs that are used to inject venom from glands located towards the rear of the upper jaws. Each of the two fangs is at the front of the mouth on a short maxillary bone that can rotate back and forth. When not in use, the fangs fold back against the roof of the mouth and are enclosed in a membranous sheath. The left and right fangs can be rotated together or independently. During a strike, the mouth can open nearly 180° and the maxilla rotates forward, erecting the fangs as late as possible so as the fangs do not become damaged. The jaws close on impact and powerful muscles that surround the venom glands contract to inject the venom as the fangs penetrate. This action is very fast; in defensive strikes it can be more a stab than a bite. Viperids use this mechanism primarily for immobilization and digestion of prey. Secondarily it is used for self-defense, though in most cases with non-prey items such as humans they are more likely to give a dry bite (not inject any venom).

Almost all vipers have keeled scales, a stocky build with a short tail, and, due to the location of the venom glands, a triangular-shaped head distinct from the neck. The great majority have vertically elliptical, or slit-shaped, pupils that can open wide to cover most of the eye or close almost completely, which helps them to see in a wide range of light levels. Typically, vipers are nocturnal and ambush their prey.

Compared to many other snakes, vipers often appear rather sluggish. Most are ovoviviparous, giving birth to live young, but a few lay eggs; the word 'viper' is derived from Latin *vivo* = 'I live' and *pario* = 'I give birth'.

Viperid snakes are found in the Americas, Africa and Eurasia. In the Americas, they are native from southern Canada south, through the United States, Mexico, Central America and into South America.The Adder branch of The Viperidae family contains the only venomous snake found in the United Kingdom. Wild viperids are not found in Australia.

Behaviour

Experiments have shown that these snakes are capable of making decisions on how much venom to inject depending on the circumstances. In all cases, the most important determinant of venom expenditure is generally the size of the snake, with larger specimens being capable of delivering much more venom. The species is also important, since some are likely to inject more venom than others, may have much venom available, strike more accurately, or deliver a number of bites in a short space of time. In predatory bites, factors that influence the amount of venom injected include the size of the prey, the species of prey, and whether the prey item is held or released. The need to label prey for chemosensory relocation after a bite and release may also play a role. In defensive bites, the amount of venom injected may be determined by the size or species of the predator (or antagonist), as well as the assessed level of threat, although larger assailants and higher threat levels may not necessarily lead to larger amounts of venom being injected.

Viperid Venoms

Viperid venoms typically contain an abundance of protein-degrading enzymes, called proteases, that produce symptoms such as pain, strong local swelling and necrosis, blood loss from cardiovascular damage complicated by coagulopathy, and disruption of the blood clotting system. Death is usually caused by collapse in blood pressure. This is in contrast to elapid venoms that generally contain neurotoxins that disable muscle contraction and cause paralysis. Death from elapid bites usually results from asphyxiation because the diaphragm can no longer contract. However, this rule does not always apply: some elapid bites include proteolytic symptoms typical of viperid bites, while some viperid bites produce neurotoxic symptoms.

Proteolytic venom is also dual-purpose: firstly, it is used for defense and to immobilize prey, as with neurotoxic venoms, secondly, many of the venom's enzymes have a digestive function, breaking down molecules in prey items, such as lipids, nucleic acids, and proteins. This is an important adaptation, as many vipers have inefficient digestive systems.

Due to the nature of proteolytic venom, a viperid bite is often a very painful experience and should always be taken seriously, even though it may not necessarily prove fatal. Even with prompt and proper treatment, a bite can still result in a permanent scar, and in the worst cases, the affected limb may even have to be amputated. A victim's fate is impossible to predict as this depends on many factors, including (but not limited to) the species and size of the snake involved, how much venom was injected (if any), and the size and condition of the patient before being bitten. Viper bite victims may also be allergic to the venom and/or the antivenom.

That Viperidae as attributed to Oppel (1811), as opposed to Laurenti (1768) or Gray (1825), is subject to some interpretation. However, the consensus among leading experts is that Laurenti used *viperae* as the plural of *vipera* (Latin for 'viper', 'adder', or 'snake') and did not intend for it to indicate a family group taxon. Rather, it is attributed to Oppel, based on his Viperini as a distinct family group name, despite the fact that Gray was the first to use the form Viperinae.

Rattlesnake

Rattlesnakes are a group of venomous snakes of the genera *Crotalus* and *Sistrurus* of the subfamily *Crotalinae* ('pit vipers'). There are 32 known species of rattlesnake, with between 65-70 subspecies.

Rattlesnakes receive their name for the rattle located at the end of their tails, which is used as a warning to passerby. The scientific name *Crotalus* derives from the Greek, meaning 'castanet'. The name *Sistrurus* is the Latinized form of the Greek word for 'tail rattler' *Seistrouros*) and shares its root with the ancient Egyptian musical instrument, the sistrum, a type of rattle.

Rattlesnakes live in diverse habitats, ranging from Southern Canada to Central Argentina. In the United States, the state with the most forms of rattlesnakes is Arizona, with seventeen species and subspecies.

Rattlesnakes are native to the Americas, with the large majority of species in the American Southwest and Mexico; Arizona has more species than any other state. Four species may be found east of the Mississippi river, and two in South America. Evidence has been collected to show the most probable ancestral area of rattlesnakes is the Sierra Madre Occidental region in Mexico. This same study found the most probable vegetation or habitat of the ancestral area to be pine-oak forests.

Ecological Role

Rattlesnakes consume mice, rats, small birds and other small animals. They lie in wait for their prey, or hunt for it in holes. The prey are killed quickly with a venomous bite as opposed to constricting. If the prey travels a bit before dying, the rattlesnake will follow it by scent.

The common kingsnake (*Lampropeltis getula*), a constrictor, is immune to the venom of rattlesnakes and other vipers, and therefore rattlesnakes form part of this snake's natural diet in the wild.

Like all pit vipers, rattlesnakes have two organs that can sense radiation: their eyes, and a set of heat-sensing 'pits' on their face that enable them to locate prey and strike towards it, based on the prey's thermal radiation signature. These pits have a relatively short effective range of approximately one ft, but nevertheless give the rattlesnake a distinctive advantage in hunting for warm-blooded creatures at night.

Rattlesnake eyes are well adapted to nocturnal use. However rattlesnakes are not exclusively nocturnal, and their vision is more acute during daylight conditions. Their eyes are capable of horizontal rotation, but they do not appear to move their eyeballs to follow moving objects.

Rattlesnakes have an exceptionally keen sense of smell. They can sense olfactory stimuli both through their nostrils, and by flicking their tongue, which carries scent-bearing particles to the Jacobson's organ in the roof of their mouth.

Rattlesnakes are born with fully functioning fangs capable of injecting venom and can regulate the amount of venom they inject when biting. Generally they deliver a full dose of venom to their prey, but may deliver less venom or none at all when biting defensively. A frightened or injured snake may not exercise such control. Young snakes are also dangerous, and should not be treated with any less caution than the adults.

Rattlesnake fangs are connected by venom ducts to large poison glands on the sides of the rear of the head. When fangs are not in use, they remain folded against the palate.

Adult rattlesnakes shed their fangs every 6-10 weeks. At least 3 pairs of replacement fangs lie behind the functional pair.

Venom

Most species of rattlesnakes have hemotoxic venom, destroying tissue, causing necrosis and coagulopathy (disrupted blood clotting). In the U.S., some varieties of the Mojave rattlesnake (*Crotalus scutulatus*) have a presynaptic neurotoxic venom component known as Mojave Type A toxin, which can cause severe paralysis.

Rattlesnake venom is a mixture of 5-15 enyzmes, various metal ions, biogenic amines, lipids, free amino acids, proteins, and polypeptides. It contains components designed to immobilize and disable the prey, as well as digestive enzymes which break down tissue to prepare for later ingestion. The venom is very stable, and retains its toxicity for many years in storage.

The rattle is composed of a series of hollow, interlocked segments made of keratin, which are created by modifying the scales that cover the tip of the tail. The contraction of special 'shaker' muscles in the tail causes these segments to vibrate against one another, making the rattling noise (which is amplified because the segments are hollow). The muscles that cause the rattle to shake are some of the fastest known, firing 50 times per second on average, sustained for up to three hours.

Each time the snake sheds its skin, a new rattle segment is added. They may shed their skins several times a year depending on food supply and growth rates. Rattlesnakes travel with their rattles held up to protect them from damage, but in spite of this their day-to-day activities in the wild still cause them to regularly break off end segments. Because of this, there is no way to determine the age of a rattlesnake based on the number of rattles on its tail.

One of the differentiating features of males and females is that males have a thicker and longer tail. The tails of males also tapers gradually from the body, whereas female tails narrows sharply at the vent.

Most rattlesnakes mate in the spring. Males will often court females, following them around during the mating season (a behaviour that is not common at other times). The males of some species, such as timber rattlesnakes (*C. horridus*), will fight each other during the mating season, in competition over females. These fights known as 'combat dances' consist of the two males intertwining the anterior portion of their bodies, often with the head and neck held vertically. The larger males usually end up driving the smaller males away.

Although many kinds of snakes and other reptiles are oviparous (lay eggs), rattlesnakes are viviparous (give birth to live young).

Rattlesnakes generally take several years to mature, and females usually reproduce only once every three years.

Rattlesnakes are the leading cause of snakebite injuries in North America, and are a significant cause in Central and South America. Rattlesnakes tend to avoid wide open spaces where they cannot hide from predators, and will generally avoid humans if they are aware of their approach.

Rattlesnakes rarely bite unless they feel threatened or provoked. A large majority of victims are males, often young and intoxicated. Approximately half of bites occur in cases where the victim saw the snake, yet made no effort to move away.

Hikers and campers should avoid contact with rattlesnakes by remaining observant and not approaching the animals. Hikers are advised to be particularly careful when negotiating fallen logs or boulders and when near rocky outcroppings and ledges where rattlesnakes may be hiding or sunning themselves. However, snakes will occasionally sun themselves in the middle of a trail, so such areas are not the only places where they are encountered. When encountering a rattlesnake on a trail, hikers are advised to keep their distance and allow the snake room to retreat.

Caution is advised even when snakes are believed to be dead; rattlesnake heads can see, flick the tongue, and inflict poisonous bites for up to an hour after being severed from the body.

Rattlesnake bites are rarely fatal to humans, if treated. Between 7,000 and 8,000 people are estimated to have been bitten by venomous snakes in the United States each year, and about five of those die. About 72 per cent of those bitten by rattlesnakes are male.

When a bite occurs, the amount of venom injected is under voluntary control by the snake. The amount released is dependent on a variety of factors including the condition of the snake (e.g. having long, healthy fangs and a full venom sack) and it's temperament (an angry, hungry snake that has just been stepped on vs. a satiated snake that was merely surprised by walking near it). Approximately 20 per cent of bites result in no envenomation at all. A lack of burning pain and edema 1 cm away from the fang marks after 1 hour, suggests that either no or minimal envenomation occured. A lack of edema or erythema in the area of the bite after 6-8 hours indicates a lack of envenomation for most rattlesnake bites.

Common symptoms include swelling, severe pain, weakness, anxiety, nausea and vomiting, hemorrhaging, perspiration, and heart failure. Local pain following envenomation is often intense, increasing with the ensuing edema.

Emergency Response

Data on the effectiveness of first aid techniques for rattlesnake bites is limited. However, general recommendations for first aid in the field are as follows:

- Remain calm, and retreat from the snake at least 10-15 feet. Arrange to have the victim transported to a medical facility as soon as possible.
- Remove restrictive clothing items (rings, bracelets, watches, buttoned shirts, etc) from the victim.
- Splint or otherwise immobilize any bitten limbs, and keep them below heart level. If (and only if) the victim is more than 1-2 hours away from a medical facility, it is recommended to place a lightly constricting band (that admits one finger beneath it) above the bitten area to prevent the systemic spread of the venom.
- Keep the victim calm; put them at rest; keep them warm and give them comfort and reassurance (which will lower their heart rate, slowing the spread of the venom). However, keeping the victim's heart rate down should never interfere with getting them to a medical facility.

- In no case should tourniquets be used, nor should any incisions or suction be applied to the wound.

Antivenom

Crotaline antivenom (or 'antivenin') is commonly used to treat the effects of local and systemic pit viper envenomations. The first step in the production of crotaline antivenom is collecting ('milking') the venom of a live rattlesnake - usually from the Western Diamondback (*Crotalus atrox*), Eastern Diamondback (*Crotalus adamanteus*), South American rattlesnake (*Crotalus durissis terrificus*), or fer-de-lance (*Bothrops atrox*). The extracted venom is then diluted and injected into horses, goats, or sheep, whose immune systems produce antibodies that protect from the toxic effects of the venom. These antibodies accumulate in the blood, which is then extracted and centrifuged to separate the red blood cells. The resulting serum is then purified into a lyophilized powder, which is packaged for distribution and later use by human patients.

Because antivenom is derived from horse serum, people generally display an allergic response during infusion.

The Feathered Serpent of the preclassic Olmec was depicted as having the combined features of the quetzal bird and rattlesnake. The Ancient Maya considered the rattlesnake to be a 'vision serpent' that acted as a conduit to the 'otherworld'.

Members of some Christian sects in the southern United States are regularly bitten when they practice 'snake handling'. Snake handling is when people hold venomous snakes, unprotected, during religious services, inspired by a literal interpretation of the Bible verse Mark 16:17-18 which reads *"In my name ... they will pick up snakes with their hands"*.

Agkistrodon Contortrix

Agkistrodon contortrix is a species of venomous snake found in North America, a member of the Crotalinae (pit viper) subfamily. Common names for the species include Copperhead and moccasin. The behaviour of *Agkistrodon contortrix* may lead to accidental encounters with humans. Five subspecies are currently recognized, including the nominate subspecies described here.

Adults usually grow to a total length of 50-95 cm (20-37 in), although some may exceed 1 m (3.3 ft). Males are usually larger than females. The maximum length reported for this species is 134.6 cm (53.0 in) for *A. c. mokasen* (Ditmars, 1931). Brimley (1944) mentions a specimen of *A. c. mokasen* from Chapel Hill, North Carolina, that was "four feet, six inches" (137.2 cm), but this may have been an approximation. The maximum length for *A. c. contortrix* is 132.1 cm (52.0 in).

The body is relatively stout and the head is broad and distinct from the neck. Because the snout slopes down and back, it appears less blunt than that of the cottonmouth, *A. piscivorus*. Consequently, the top of the head extends further forward than the mouth.

The scalation includes 21-25 (usually 23) rows of dorsal scales at midbody, 138-157 ventral scales in both sexes and 38-62/37-57 subcaudal scales in males/females. The subcaudals are usually single, but the percentage thereof decreases clinally from the northeast, where about 80 per cent are undivided, to the southwest of the geographic range where as little as 50 per cent may be undivided. On the head there are usually 9 large symmetrical plates, 6-10 (usually 8) supralabial scales and 8-13 (usually 10) sublabial scales.

The colour pattern consists of a pale tan to pinkish tan ground colour that becomes darker towards the midline, overlaid with a series of 10-18 (13.4) crossbands. Characteristically, both the ground colour and crossband pattern are pale in *A.c. contortrix*. These crossbands are light tan to pinkish tan to pale brown in the center, but darker towards the edges. They are about 2 scales wide or less at the midline of the back, but expand to a width of 6-10 scales on the sides of the body. They do not extend down to the ventral scales. Often, the crossbands are divided at the midline and alternate on either side of the body, with some individuals even having more half bands than complete ones.

A series of dark brown spots is also present on the flanks, next to the belly, and are largest and darkest in the spaces between the crossbands. The belly is the same colour as the ground colour, but may be a little whitish in part. At the base of the tail there are 1-3 (usually 2) brown crossbands followed by a gray area. In juveniles, the pattern on the tail is more distinct: 7-9 crossbands are visible, while the tip is yellow. On the head, the crown is usually unmarked, except for a pair of small dark spots, one near the midline of each parietal scale. A faint postocular stripe is also present; diffuse above and bordered below by a narrow brown edge.

Several aberrant colour patterns for *A.c. contortrix*, or populations that intergrade with it, have also been reported. In a specimen described by Livezey (1949) from Walker County, Texas, 11 of 17 crossbands were not joined middorsally, while on one side three of the crossbands were fused together longitudinally to form a continuous undulating band, surmounted above by a dark stripe that was 2-2.5 scales wide. In another specimen, from Lowndes County, Alabama, the first three crossbands were complete, followed by a dark stripe that ran down either side of the body, with points of pigment reaching up to the midline in six places but never getting there, after which the last four crossbands on the tail were also complete. A specimen found in Terrebonne Parish, Louisiana by Ernest A. Liner, had a similar striped pattern, with only the first and last two crossbands being normal.

Copperhead (snake), chunk head, death adder, highland moccasin, (dry-land) moccasin, narrow-banded copperhead, northern copperhead, pilot snake, poplar leaf, red oak, red snake, southeastern copperhead, white oak snake, American copperhead, southern copperhead, cantil cobrizo (Spanish).

Geographic Range

Found in the United States in the states of Texas, Oklahoma, Kansas, Missouri, Arkansas, Louisiana, Mississippi, Alabama, Georgia, Florida, South Carolina, North Carolina, Tennessee, Kentucky, Virginia, West Virginia, Illinois, Indiana, Ohio, Iowa, Pennsylvania, Maryland, New Jersey, Delaware,

New York, Connecticut and Massachusetts. In Mexico it occurs in Chihuahua and Coahuila. The type locality is 'Carolina'. Schmidt (1953) proposed that the type locality be restricted to 'Charleston, South Carolina'.

Unlike some other species of North American pit vipers (*Crotalus horridus* and *Sistrurus catenatus*), *Agkistrodon contortrix* has not reestablished itself north of the terminal moraine after the last glacial period (the Wisconsin glaciation).

Habitat

Within its range it occupies a variety of different habitats. In most of North America it favors deciduous forest and mixed woodlands. It is often associated with rock outcroppings and ledges, but is also found in low-lying swampy regions. In the states around the Gulf of Mexico, however, this species is also found in coniferous forest. In the Chihuahuan Desert of west Texas and northern Mexico, it occurs in riparian habitats, usually near permanent or semipermanent water and sometimes in dry arroyos (brooks).

Like all pit vipers, *A. contortrix* is generally an ambush predator: it takes up a promising position and waits for suitable prey to arrive. One exception to ambush foraging occurs when copperheads feed on insects such as caterpillars and freshly molted cicadas. When hunting insects, copperheads actively pursue their prey. Juveniles use a brightly coloured tail to attract frogs and perhaps lizards, a behaviour termed caudal luring (see video: . In the southern United States, they are nocturnal during the hot summer months, but are commonly active during the day during the spring and fall.

Like most North American viperids, these snakes prefer to avoid humans and, given the opportunity, will leave the area without biting. However, unlike other viperids they will often 'freeze' instead of slithering away, and as a result many bites occur from people unknowingly stepping on or near them. This tendency to freeze likely evolved because of the extreme effectiveness of their camouflage. When lying on dead leaves or red clay they can be almost impossible to notice. They will frequently stay still even when approached closely, and will generally strike only if physical contact is made.

Roughly 90 per cent of its diet consists of small rodents, such as mice and voles. They have also shown fondness for large insects and frogs, and though highly terrestrial, have been known to climb trees to gorge on emerging cicadas.

Reproduction

A. contortrix breeds in late summer, but not every year: sometimes a female will produce young for several years running, then not breed at all for a time. They give birth to live young about 20 cm long: a typical litter is 4 to 7, but it can be as few as one or as many as 20. Their size apart, the young are similar to the adults, but lighter in colour, and with a yellow-marked tip to the tail, which is used to lure lizards and frogs.

A study has shown that *A. contortrix* males have longer tongue tine lengths than females during the breeding season which may aid in chemoreception of males searching for females.

Venom

Although venomous, these snakes are generally non-aggressive and bites are almost never fatal. Copperhead venom has an estimated lethal dose of around 100 mg, and tests on mice show its potency is among the lowest of all pit vipers, and slightly weaker than that of its close relative, the cottonmouth. Copperheads often employ a 'warning bite' when stepped on or agitated and inject a relatively small amount of venom, if any at all. 'Dry bites' involving no venom are particularly common with the copperhead, though all pit vipers are capable of a dry bite.

Bite symptoms include intense pain, tingling, throbbing, swelling, and severe nausea. Damage can occur to muscle and bone tissue, especially when the bite occurs in the outer extremities such as the hands and feet, areas in which there is not a large muscle mass to absorb the venom. A bite from any venomous snake should be taken very seriously and immediate medical attention sought, as allergic reaction and secondary infection are always possible.

The venom of the Southern copperhead has been found to hold a protein called 'Contortrostatin' that halts the growth of cancer cells and also stops the migration of the tumors to other sites. It will probably be ten or more years before contortrostatin is used in practical treatment but it has shown to be a very promising drug in laboratory studies.

Lachesis

Lachesis is a genus of venomous pitvipers found in remote forested areas of Central and South America. The generic name refers to one of the Three Fates in Greek mythology who determined the length of the thread of life. Three species are currently recognized.

Adults vary in length from 2 to 2.5 m (6.5 to 8.25 ft), although some may grow to as much as 3 m (10 ft). The largest known specimen was just under 3.65 m (12 ft), making it the longest venomous snake in the Western Hemisphere. This is also the longest viper, though not the heaviest (it is surpassed by the gaboon viper and the Eastern diamondback rattlesnake). The bushmaster's tail ends with a horny spine which it sometimes vibrates when disturbed in a similar manner to rattlesnakes. This led to some calling it 'the mute rattlesnake'.

Geographic Range

Found in Central and South America. Also found on the island of Trinidad.

Reproduction

Bushmasters lay eggs: about a dozen in an average clutch. The female reportedly remains with her eggs during incubation and may aggressively defend the nest if approached. The hatchlings average 30 cm in length and are more colourful than the adults. *Lachesis* is thought to be unique among New World pit vipers in laying eggs rather than giving birth to live young, although some evidence suggests that the species *Bothrocophias colombianus* found in Colombia may do the same.

One of the largest and most dangerous snakes in South America, this snake is capable of multiple- bite strikes and the injection of large amounts of venom. Even the bite of a juvenile specimen can be fatal.

Campbell and Lamar (2004) also recognize a fourth species, *L. acrochorda*, referring to it as the Chochoan bushmaster. It is found in western Panama and northwestern Colombia and Ecuador. Its evolutionary relationships are not certain, but *Lachesis acrochorda* is thought to be closer to the South American bushmaster *L. muta* than to the two Central American species *L. stenophrys* and *L. melanocephala*.

Cultural Depictions

The bushmaster snake is the antagonist in the tenth show of the old time radio show *Escape*. The show's title was "A Shipment of Mute Fate", and starred Jack Webb and Raymond Lawrence. It was broadcast on 15 October 1947. The story was also adapted for Suspense starring Jack Kelly, broadcast on January 6, 1957. The bushmaster is referenced in the film *Romancing the Stone*.

10 Colubrid

A colubrid (from Latin *coluber*, snake) is a member of the snake family Colubridae. This broad classification of snakes includes about two-thirds of all snake species on earth. Colubrid species are found on every continent except Antarctica.

While most colubrids are nonvenomous (or have venom that is not known to be harmful to humans) and are mostly harmless, a few groups, such as genus *Boiga*, can produce medically significant bites, while the boomslang, the twig snakes and the Asian genus *Rhabdophis* have caused human fatalities.

Some colubrids are described as opisthoglyphous, meaning they have elongated, grooved teeth located in the back of the upper jaw. The opisthoglyphous dentition apears at least two times in the history of snakes. These are unlike those of vipers and elapids that are located in the front.

The Colubridae are not a natural group, as many are more closely related to other groups, such as elapids, than to each other. This family has classically been a garbage bin taxon for snakes that do not fit elsewhere. Ongoing research, hopefully, will sort out the relations within this group.

Subfamily Boodontinae

- *Bothrolycus*
- *Bothrophthalmus*
- *Buhoma* (tentatively placed here)
- *Chamaelycus*

- *Dendrolycus*
- *Dipsina*
- *Dromophis*
- *Duberria* (tentatively placed here)
- *Gonionotophis*
- *Grayia*
- *Hormonotus*
- *Lamprophis*
- *Lycodonomorphus*
- *Lycophidion*
- *Macroprotodon*
- *Mehelya*
- *Montaspis* (tentatively placed here)
- *Pseudaspis*
- *Pseudoboodon*
- *Pythonodipsas*
- *Scaphiophis*

Subfamily Calamariinae

- *Calamaria*
- *Calamorhabdium*
- *Collorhabdium*
- *Etheridgeum*
- *Macrocalamus*
- *Pseudorabdion*
- *Rabdion*

Subfamily Colubrinae

- Nearly 100 genera

Subfamily Dipsadinae

- *Adelphicos*
- *Amastridium*
- *Atractus*
- *Calamodontophis* (tentatively placed here)
- *Carphophis* (tentatively placed here)

- *Chersodromus*
- *Coniophanes*
- *Contia* (tentatively placed here)
- *Crisantophis* (tentatively placed here)
- *Cryophis*
- *Diadophis* (tentatively placed here)
- *Diaphorolepsis* (tentatively placed here)
- *Dipsas*
- *Echinanthera* (tentatively placed here)
- *Emmochliophis* (tentatively placed here)
- *Enuliophis* (tentatively placed here)
- *Enulius* (tentatively placed here)
- *Eridiphas*
- *Geophis*
- *Gomesophis* (tentatively placed here)
- *Hydromorphus* (tentatively placed here)
- *Hypsiglena*
- *Imantodes*
- *Leptodeira*
- *Ninia*
- *Nothopsis* (tentatively placed here)
- *Pliocercus*
- *Pseudoleptodeira*
- *Pseudotomodon* (tentatively placed here)
- *Ptychophis* (tentatively placed here)
- *Rhadinaea*
- *Rhadinophanes* (tentatively placed here)
- *Sibon*
- *Sibynomorphus*
- *Synophis* (tentatively placed here)
- *Tachymenis* (tentatively placed here)
- *Taeniophallus* (tentatively placed here)
- *Tantalophis* (tentatively placed here)

- *Thamnodynastes* (tentatively placed here)
- *Tomodon* (tentatively placed here)
- *Tretanorhinus*
- *Trimetopon*
- *Tropidodipsas*
- *Urotheca*
- *Xenopholis* (tentatively placed here)

Subfamily Homalopsinae

- About 10 genera

Subfamily Natricinae

- About 30 genera

Subfamily Pareatinae

- Three genera

Subfamily Psammophiinae

- *Hemirhagerrhis*
- *Malpolon*
- *Mimophis*
- *Psammophis*
- *Psammophylax*
- *Rhamphiophis*

Subfamily Pseudoxenodontinae

- *Plagiopholis*
- *Pseudoxenodon*

Subfamily Pseudoxyrhophiinae

- About 20 genera

Subfamily Xenodermatinae

- *Achalinus*
- *Fimbrios*
- *Oxyrhabdium*
- *Stoliczkaia*
- *Xenodermus*
- *Xylophis*

Subfamily Xenodontinae

- Some 55-60 genera
- *incertae sedis*
- *Blythia*
- *Cercaspis*
- *Cyclocorus*
- *Elapoidis*
- *Gongylosoma*
- *Haplocercus*
- *Helophis*
- *Myersophis*
- *Omoadiphas* (recently discovered)
- *Oreocalamus*
- *Poecilopholis*
- *Rhabdops*
- *Tetralepis*
- *Thermophis*
- *Trachischium*

Ahaetulla

Ahaetulla is a genus of colubrid snakes commonly referred to as vine snakes, or whip snakes. They are found predominantly from Sri Lanka, India through to Korea and much of southeast Asia, including many Pacific islands. They are mildly venomous and what is commonly termed as 'rear-fanged' or more appropriately, opisthoglyphous, meaning their enlarged teeth or fangs intended to aid in venom delivery are located in the back of the upper jaw, instead of in the front like they are in vipers or cobras.

The taxonomy of vine snakes is not well documented, and literature varies widely, but there are eight commonly accepted species in the genus *Ahaetulla*:

- Günther's Vine Snake or Indian Bronzeback, *Ahaetulla dispar* (Günther, 1864)
- Speckle-headed Whipsnake, *Ahaetulla fasciolata* (Fischer, 1885)

- Burmese Vine Snake, *Ahaetulla fronticincta* (Günther, 1858)
- Malayan Green Whipsnake, *Ahaetulla mycterizans* (Linnaeus, 1758)
- Long-nosed Whip Snake, *Ahaetulla nasuta* (La Cépède, 1789)
- Western Ghats Bronzeback, *Ahaetulla perroteti* (Duméril & Bibron, 1854)
- Oriental Whipsnake or Asian Vine Snake, *Ahaetulla prasina* (Shaw, 1802)
- *Ahaetulla prasina prasina* (Boie, 1827)
- *Ahaetulla prasina medioxima* (Lazell, 2002)
- *Ahaetulla prasina preocularis* (Taylor, 1922)
- *Ahaetulla prasina suluensis* (Gaulke, 1994)
- Brown-speckled Whipsnake, *Ahaetulla pulverulenta* (Duméril & Bibron, 1854)

All *Ahaetulla* species are characterized by thin, elongated bodies, with extremely long tails and a sharply triangular shaped head. They are primarily green in colour, but can vary quite a bit to yellows, oranges, greys, and browns. They can have black and/or white patterning, or can be solid in colour. Their eyes are unique in the reptile world, having keen binocular vision and keyhole shaped pupils.

Behaviour

They are primarily diurnal and arboreal, living in humid rainforests. Their diet consists mainly of lizards, but sometimes frogs and rodents are also consumed. *Ahaetulla fronticincta*, however, feeds exclusively on fish, striking its prey from branches overhanging water. *Ahaetulla* venom is not considered to be dangerous to humans, but serves to cause paralysis in their fast moving prey choices. They are ovoviviparous.

In Captivity

Ahaetulla species are frequently imported into the exotic pet trade. They are difficult to care for, requiring a humid arboreal habitat and a diet of lizards as they rarely switch to rodents. They also stress easily, are prone to skin infections, and internal parasites.

Boomslang

A boomslang (*Dispholidus typus*) is a relatively small, venomous colubrid snake native to sub-Saharan Africa. It is currently the only species in its genus, although several species and subspecies have been described in the past. Its name means 'tree snake' in Afrikaans and Dutch (*boom* meaning 'tree' (a cognate of 'beam', which means a long and large piece of wood, generally a support in a building), and *slang* meaning 'snake'). In Afrikaans, the name is pronounced . The snake is thought to be closely related to members of the genera *Thelotornis, Thrasops, Rhamnophis,* and *Xyelodontophis,* with which it forms the tribe Dispholidini.

Boomslangs are oviparous. The eggs have a relatively long (3 months on average) incubation period. Hatchlings are greyish with blue speckles. They attain their adult colouration after several years.

Behaviour and Diet

Boomslangs are diurnal and largely arboreal. Their diet includes chameleons and other arboreal lizards, frogs, and occasionally small mammals, birds, and eggs from nesting birds, all of which they swallow whole. During cool weather, they will hibernate for moderate periods, often curling up inside the enclosed nests of birds such as weavers.

Venom

Many members of the family Colubridae considered venomous are essentially harmless to humans, because they either have small venom glands, relatively weak venom, or an inefficient system for delivery of venom. However, the boomslang is a notable exception in that it has a highly potent venom, which it delivers through large fangs that are located in the rear of the jaw. In order for the bite to take place the Boomslang's jaw will open at a 90 degree angle. The venom of the boomslang is primarily a hemotoxin; it disables the blood clotting process and the victim may well die as a result of internal and external bleeding. Other signs and symptoms include headache, nausea, sleepiness and mental disorders.

Because the venom is slow to act, symptoms may not be manifest until many hours after the bite. On one hand, this provides time for procuring the antivenin, while on the other it may lead victims to underestimate the seriousness of the bite. Snakes of any species may sometimes fail to inject venom when they bite, so after a few hours without any noticeable effects, victims of boomslang bites may believe (wrongly) their injury is not serious.

An adult boomslang has 1.6-8 mg of venom. Various sources give figures ranging from 0.06-0.72 mg/kg being sufficient to kill mice in 50 per cent of cases, if the venom reaches a vein (LD50).

In 1957, well-known herpetologist Karl Schmidt died after being bitten by a boomslang. D.S. Chapman states that between 1919 and 1962 there were eight serious human envenomations by boomslangs, two of which were fatal. The South African Vaccine Producers (formerly South African Institute of Medical Research) manufactures a monovalent antivenin for use in boomslang envenomations.

The boomslang is a timid snake, and bites generally occur only when people attempt to handle, catch or kill the animal. The above data suggest boomslangs are unlikely to be a significant source of human fatalities throughout their distribution range.

Shredded skin of a boomslang is one of the ingredients to make the Polyjuice Potion in J.K. Rowling's *Harry Potter and the Chamber of Secrets.*

The venom of the boomslang also features in the Agatha Christie thriller, *Death in the Clouds* (pub.1935), featuring her famous detective, Hercule Poirot.

In Stephen King's short story, "Autopsy Room Four", the main character is bitten by a fictional snake called a "Peruvian boomslang". King says he got the name from *Death in the Clouds*, mentioned above.

A distillation of boomslang venom is combined with dimethyl sulfoxide to create a contact poison that is the murder weapon in an episode of *Quincy, ME.*

A character named Boomslang is a Marvel Comics supervillain.

In *A King's Trade* by Dewey Lambdin, one of Captain Alan Lewrie's black sailors runs away while anchored in South Africa and is killed by a boomslang.

A popular jungle, dub-step and drum and bass night is hosted at the Junction, Cambridge.

Boomslang is the title of a 2003 album by former Smiths guitarist and songwriter Johnny Marr, credited to Johnny Marr and the Healers.

A computer mouse named after the snake, also called the Boomslang, is manufactured by the Razer Company, Ltd.

Boiga

Boiga is a large genus of mildly venomous, rear-fanged, colubrid snakes typically known as the cat-eyed snakes or just cat snakes. They are primarily found throughout southeast Asia, India and Australia, but due to their extremely hardy nature and adaptability have spread to many other suitable habitats around the world. There are thirty-three recognized species in the genus.

- Andaman cat snake, *Boiga andamanensis* (Wall, 1909)
- Leyte cat snake, *Boiga angulata* (Peters, 1861)
- Barnes' cat snake, *Boiga barnesii* (Günther, 1869)
- Beddome's cat snake, *Boiga beddomei* (Wall, 1909)
- *Boiga bengkuluensis* (Orlov, Kudryavtzev, Ryabov & Shumakov, 2003)
- Blandings tree snake, *Boiga blandingii* (Hallowell, 1844)
- *Boiga bourreti* (Tillack, Ziegler & Le Khac Quyet, 2004)
- Sri Lanka cat Snake, *Boiga ceylonensis* (Günther, 1858)
- green cat snake, *Boiga cyanea* (Duméril, Bibron & Duméril, 1854)
- dog-toothed cat snake, *Boiga cynodon* (Boie, 1827)
- gold-ringed cat snake or mangrove snake, *Boiga dendrophila*
- *Boiga dendrophila annectens* (Boulenger, 1896)
- *Boiga dendrophila dendrophila* (Boie, 1827)

- *Boiga dendrophila divergens* (Taylor, 1922)
- *Boiga dendrophila gemmicincta* (Duméril, Bibron & Duméril, 1854)
- *Boiga dendrophila latifasciata* (Boulenger, 1896)
- *Boiga dendrophila levitoni* (Gaulke, Demegillo & Vogel, 2005)
- *Boiga dendrophila melanota* (Boulenger, 1896)
- *Boiga dendrophila multicincta* (Boulenger, 1896)
- *Boiga dendrophila occidentalis* (Brongersma, 1934)
- Pirmad cat snake, *Boiga dightoni* (Boulenger, 1894)
- white-spotted cat snake, *Boiga drapiezii* (Boie & Boie, 1827)
- Forsten's cat snake, *Boiga forsteni* (Duméril, Bibron & Duméril, 1854)
- Arrowback tree snake, *Boiga gokool* (Gray, 1835)
- Boiga guangxiensis (Wen, 1998)
- Brown tree snake, *Boiga irregularis* (Merrem, 1802)
- jasper cat snake, *Boiga jaspidea* (Duméril, Bibron & Duméril, 1854)
- Kelung cat snake, *Boiga kraepelini* (Stejneger, 1902)
- Many-banded tree snake, *Boiga multifasciata* (Blyth, 1861)
- Many-spotted cat snake, *Boiga multomaculata* (Boie, 1827)
- Black-headed cat snake, *Boiga nigriceps* (Günther, 1863)
- *Boiga nuchalis* (Günther, 1875)
- Tawny cat snake, *Boiga ochracea* (Günther, 1868)
- Philippine cat snake, *Boiga philippina* (Peters, 1867)
- Fischer's cat snake, *Boiga pulverulenta* (Fischer, 1856)
- *Boiga quincunciata* (Wall, 1908)
- Banded cat snake , *Boiga saengsomi* (Nutafand, 1985)
- Schultz's blunt-headed tree snake *Boiga schultzei* (Taylor, 1923)
- Gray cat snake, *Boiga siamensis* (Nootpand, 1971)
- *Boiga tanahjampeana* (Orlov & Ryabov, 2002)
- Indian gamma snake, *Boiga trigonata*
- *Boiga trigonata trigonata* (Schneider, 1802)
- *Boiga trigonata melanocephala* (Annandale, 1904)
- Nicobar cat snake, *Boiga wallachi* Das, 1998

- Ranawana's golden cat snake, *Boiga ranawanei* (Samarawickrama, Samarawickrama, Wijesena & Orlov, 2006 (2005)

Description and Behaviour

Cat snakes are typically thin, long-bodied snakes with large heads and large eyes. They vary greatly in pattern and colour. Many species have banding, but some are spotted and some are solid coloured. Colours are normally black, brown, or green with white or yellow accents.

They are primarily arboreal, nocturnal snakes that prey on various species of lizards, birds, and rodents. Their venom toxicity varies from species to species, but is not generally considered to be life threatening to humans. *Boiga* species are oviparous.

In Captivity

Boiga dendrophila is by far the most common species in captivity, but *Boiga cynea* and *Boiga nigriceps* are also found. Others are not commonly available. They are hardy and adaptable and tend to do well in captivity after the initial period of stress from the importation process is passed. They are not bred commonly in captivity, so most specimens available are wild caught, and thus are prone to heavy internal parasite load. Adjusting them to a rodent only diet can be difficult for the inexperienced reptile keeper.

Invasive Species

Boiga irregularis in particular has been federally banned in the United States because of its effect by accidentally being introduced to the island of Guam. Some time during the 1950s, these snakes (or possibly a single female with eggs) reached the island, possibly having hidden in imported plant pots. The island of Guam lacks native snakes or predators that can deal with snakes the size and aggressiveness of *Boiga irregularis*. As a result, they have bred unchecked as an invasive species, and began consuming the island's bird life in extreme numbers. Currently, dozens of bird species have been completely eradicated from the island, many species that were found nowhere else on earth, and the snake has reached astonishing population densities, reported to be as high as 15,000 snakes per square mile. In addition to devouring the native fauna, this species will routinely crawl into power transformers, and, unfortunately for all involved, this typically results in both an electrocuted snake and substantial blackouts.

Sidewinding

Sidewinding is a type of locomotion unique to caenophidian snakes, used to move across loose or slippery substrates. It is most often used by the Saharan horned viper, *Cerastes cerastes,* and the sidewinder rattlesnake, *Crotalus cerastes,* to move across loose desert sands, but it is also used by Homalopsine snakes in Southeast Asia to move across tidal mud flats. Any number of caenophidian snakes can be induced to sidewind on artificial smooth surfaces, though difficulty in getting them to do so and their proficiency at it vary greatly.

The method of movement is derived from lateral undulation, and is very similar, in spite of appearances. A picture of a snake performing lateral undulation would show something like a sine wave, with straight segments of the body having either a positive or negative slope. Sidewinding is accomplished by simply lifting all the segments with the same slope off the ground.

In the resultant movement, the snake's body is always in static (as opposed to sliding) contact when touching the ground. The head seems to be "thrown" forward, and the body follows, being lifted from the prior position and moved forward to lie on the ground ahead of where it was originally. Meanwhile, the head is being thrown forward again. In this way, the snake slowly progresses at an angle, leaving a series of mostly straight, J-shaped tracks. Because the snake's body is in static contact with the ground, imprints of the belly scales can be seen in the tracks, and each track is almost exactly as long as the snake.

Below is a crude animated line-drawing showing the locomotor pattern of sidewinding. The light brown areas are the tracks left behind, and also indicate where the body of the snake touched the ground.

11 The Dangerous Snakebite

A snakebite is an injury caused by a bite from a snake, often resulting in puncture wounds inflicted by the animal's fangs and sometimes resulting in envenomation. Although the majority of snake species are non-venomous and typically kill their prey with constriction rather than venom, venomous snakes can be found on every continent except Antarctica. Snakes often bite their prey as a method of hunting, but also for defensive purposes against predators. Since the physical appearance of snakes may differ, there is often no practical way to identify a species and professional medical attention should be sought.

The outcome of snake bites depends on numerous factors, including the species of snake, the area of the body bitten, the amount of venom injected, and the health conditions of the victim. Feelings of terror and panic are common after a snakebite and can produce a characteristic set of symptoms mediated by the autonomic nervous system, such as a racing heart and nausea. Bites from non-venomous snakes can also cause injury, often due to lacerations caused by the snake's teeth, or from a resulting infection. A bite may also trigger an anaphylactic reaction, which is potentially fatal. First aid recommendations for bites depend on the snakes inhabiting the region, as effective treatments for bites inflicted by some species can be ineffective for others.

The number of fatalities attributed to snake bites varies greatly by geographical area. Although deaths are relatively rare in Australia, Europe and North America, the morbidity and mortality associated with snake bites is a serious public health problem in many regions of the world, particularly in rural areas lacking medical facilities. Further, while South Asia, Southeast Asia, and sub-Saharan Africa report the highest number of bites, there is also a high incidence in the Neotropics and other equatorial and subtropical regions. Each year tens of thousands of people die from snake bites, yet the risk of being bitten can be lowered with preventive measures, such as wearing protective footwear and avoiding areas known to be inhabited by dangerous snakes.

The most common symptoms of all snakebites are overwhelming fear, panic, and emotional instability, which may cause symptoms such as nausea and vomiting, diarrhea, vertigo, fainting, tachycardia, and cold, clammy skin. Television, literature, and folklore are in part responsible for the hype surrounding snakebites, and a victim may have unwarranted thoughts of imminent death.

Dry snakebites, and those inflicted by a non-venomous species, can still cause severe injury to the victim. There are several reasons for this: a snakebite which is not treated properly may become infected (as is often reported by the victims of viper bites whose fangs are capable of inflicting deep puncture wounds), the bite may cause anaphylaxis in certain people, and the snake's saliva and fangs may harbor many dangerous microbial contaminants, including *Clostridium tetani*. If neglected, an infection may spread and potentially kill the victim.

Most snakebites, whether by a venomous snake or not, will have some type of local effect. There is minor pain and redness in over 90 per cent of cases, although this varies depending on the site. Bites by vipers and some cobras may be extremely painful, with the local tissue sometimes becoming tender and severely swollen within five minutes. This area may also bleed and blister and can eventually lead to tissue necrosis. Other common initial symptoms of pitviper and viper bites include lethargy, bleeding, weakness, nausea, and vomiting. Symptoms may become more life-threatening over time, developing into hypotension, tachypnea, severe tachycardia, severe internal bleeding, altered sensorium, kidney failure and respiratory failure.

Interestingly, bites caused by the Mojave rattlesnake, kraits, coral snake, and the speckled rattlesnake reportedly cause little or no pain despite being serious injuries. Victims may also describe a 'rubbery', 'minty', or 'metallic' taste if bitten by certain species of rattlesnake. Spitting cobras and rinkhalses can spit venom in their victims' eyes. This results in immediate pain, ophthalmoparesis, and sometimes blindness.

Some Australian elapids and most viper envenomations will cause coagulopathy, sometimes so severe that a person may bleed spontaneously from the mouth, nose, and even old, seemingly-healed wounds. Internal organs may bleed, including the brain and intestines and will cause ecchymosis (bruising) of the victim's skin.

Venom emitted from elapids, including sea snakes, kraits, cobras, king cobra, mambas, and many Australian species, contain toxins which attack the nervous system, causing neurotoxicity. The victim may present with strange disturbances to their vision, including blurriness. Paresthesia throughout the body, as well as difficulty speaking and breathing, may be reported. Nervous system problems will cause a huge array of symptoms, and those provided here are not exhaustive. If the victim is not treated immediately they may die from respiratory failure.

Venom emitted from some types of cobras, almost all vipers, some Australian elapids and some sea snakes causes necrosis of muscle tissue. Muscle tissue will begin to die throughout the body, a condition known as rhabdomyolysis. Rhabdomyolysis can result in damage to the kidneys as a result of myoglobin accumulation in the renal tubules. This, coupled with hypotension, can lead to acute renal failure, and, if left untreated, eventually death.

Since envenomation is completely voluntary, all venomous snakes are capable of biting without injecting venom into their victim. Snakes may deliver such a "dry bite" rather than waste their venom on a creature too large for them to eat. However, the percentage of dry bites varies between species: 50 per cent of bites from the normally timid coral snake do not result in envenomation, whereas only 25 per cent of pitviper bites are dry. Furthermore, some snake genera, such as rattlesnakes, significantly increase the amount of venom injected in defensive bites compared to predatory strikes.

Some dry bites may also be the result of imprecise timing on the snake's part, as venom may be prematurely released before the fangs have penetrated the victim's flesh. Even without venom, some snakes, particularly large constrictors such as those belonging to the Boidae and Pythonidae families, can deliver damaging bites; large specimens often cause severe lacerations as the victim or the snake itself pull away, causing the flesh to be torn by the needle-sharp recurved teeth embedded in the victim. While not as life-threatening as a bite from a venomous species, the bite can be at least temporarily debilitating and could lead to dangerous infections if improperly dealt with.

While most snakes must open their mouths before biting, African and Middle Eastern snakes belonging to the family Atractaspididae are able to fold their fangs to the side of their head without opening their mouth and jab at victims.

It has been suggested that snakes evolved the mechanisms necessary for venom formation and delivery sometime during the Miocene epoch. During the mid-Tertiary, most snakes were large ambush predators belonging to the superfamily Henophidia, which use constriction to kill their prey. As open grasslands replaced forested areas in parts of the world, some snake families evolved to become smaller and thus more agile. However, subduing and killing prey became more difficult for the smaller snakes, leading to the evolution of snake venom. Other research on Toxicofera, a hypothetical clade thought to be ancestral to most living reptiles, suggests an earlier time frame for the evolution of snake venom, possibly to the order of tens of millions of years, during the Late Cretaceous.

Snake venom is produced in modified parotid glands normally responsible for secreting saliva. It is stored in structures called alveoli behind the animal's eyes, and ejected voluntarily through its hollow tubular fangs. Venom is composed of hundreds to thousands of different proteins and enzymes, all serving a variety of purposes, such as interfering with a prey's cardiac system or increasing tissue permeability so that venom is absorbed faster.

Venom in many snakes, such as pitvipers, affects virtually every organ system in the human body and can be a combination of many toxins, including cytotoxins, hemotoxins, neurotoxins, and myotoxins, allowing for an enormous variety of symptoms. Earlier, the venom of a particular snake was considered to be one kind only i.e. either hemotoxic or neurotoxic, and this erroneous belief may still persist wherever the updated literature is hard to access. Although there is much known about the protein compositions of venoms from Asian and American snakes, comparatively little is known of Australian snakes.

The strength of venom differs markedly between species and even more so between families, as measured by LD_{50} in mice. Subcutaneous LD_{50} varies by over 140-fold within elapids and by more than 100-fold in vipers. The amount of venom produced also differs among species, with the Gaboon viper able to potentially deliver from 450-600mg of venom in a single bite, the most of any snake. Opisthoglyphous colubrids have venom ranging from life-threatening (in the case of the boomslang) to barely noticeable.

Snakes are most likely to bite when they feel threatened, are startled, are provoked, or have no means of escape when cornered. Encountering a snake is always considered dangerous and it is recommended to leave the vicinity. There is no practical way to safely identify any snake species as appearances may vary dramatically.

Snakes are likely to approach residential areas when attracted by prey, such as rodents. Practicing regular pest control can reduce the threat of snakes considerably. It is beneficial to know the species of snake that are common in local areas, or while traveling or hiking. Areas of the world such as Africa, Australia, the Neotropics, and southern Asia are inhabited by many highly dangerous species. Being wary of snake presence and ultimately avoiding it when known is strongly recommended.

When in the wilderness, treading heavily creates ground vibrations and noise, which will often cause snakes to flee from the area. However, this generally only applies to North America as some larger and more aggressive snakes in other parts of the world, such as king cobras and black mambas, will protect their territory. When dealing with direct encounters it is best to remain silent and motionless. If the snake has not yet fled it is important to step away slowly and cautiously.

The use of a flashlight when engaged in camping activities, such as gathering firewood at night, can be helpful. Snakes may also be unusually active during especially warm nights when ambient temperatures exceed 21°C (70°F). It is advised not to reach blindly into hollow logs, flip over large rocks, and enter old cabins or other potential snake hiding-places. When rock climbing, it is not safe to grab ledges or crevices without examining them first, as snakes are cold-blooded and often sunbathe atop rock ledges.

Pet owners of domestic animals or snakes should be aware that a snake is capable of causing injury and that is necessary to always act with caution. When handling snakes it is never wise to consume alcoholic beverages. In the United States more than 40 per cent of snakebite victims intentionally put themselves in harm's way by attempting to capture wild snakes or by carelessly handling their dangerous pets—40 per cent of that number had a blood alcohol level of 0.1 percent or more.

It is also important to avoid snakes that appear to be dead, as some species will actually roll over on their backs and stick out their tongue to fool potential threats. A snake's detached head can immediately act by reflex and potentially bite. The induced bite can be just as severe as that of a live snake. Dead snakes are also incapable of regulating the venom they inject, so a bite from a dead snake can often contain large amounts of venom.

Treatment

It is not an easy task determining whether or not a bite by any species of snake is life-threatening. A bite by a North American copperhead on the ankle is usually a moderate injury to a healthy adult, but a bite to a child's abdomen or face by the same snake may be fatal. The outcome of all snakebites depends on a multitude of factors: the size, physical condition, and temperature of the snake, the age and physical condition of the victim, the area and tissue bitten (e.g., foot, torso, vein or muscle), the amount of venom injected, the time it takes for the patient to find treatment, and finally the quality of that treatment.

Snake Identification

Identification of the snake is important in planning treatment in certain areas of the world, but is not always possible. Ideally the dead snake would be brought in with the patient, but in areas where snake bite is more common, local knowledge may be sufficient to recognize the snake. However, in regions where polyvalent antivenoms are available, such as North America, identification of snake is not a high priority item.

The three types of venomous snakes that cause the majority of major clinical problems are vipers, kraits, and cobras. Knowledge of what species are present locally can be crucial, as is knowledge of typical signs and symptoms of envenomation by each type of snake. A scoring systems can be used to try and determine the biting snake based on clinical features, but these scoring systems are extremely specific to particular geographical areas.

First Aid

Snakebite first aid recommendations vary, in part because different snakes have different types of venom. Some have little local effect, but life-threatening systemic effects, in which case containing the venom in the region of the bite by pressure immobilization is highly desirable. Other venoms instigate localized tissue damage around the bitten area, and immobilization may increase the severity of the damage in this area, but also reduce the total area affected; whether this trade-off is desirable remains a point of controversy.

Because snakes vary from one country to another, first aid methods also vary. As always, this article is not a legitimate substitute for professional medical advice. Readers are strongly advised to obtain guidelines from a reputable first aid organisation in their own region, and to be wary of homegrown or anecdotal remedies.

However, most first aid guidelines agree on the following:

- Protect the patient (and others, including yourself) from further bites. While identifying the species is desirable in certain regions, do not risk further bites or delay proper medical treatment by attempting to capture or kill the snake. If the snake has not already fled, carefully remove the victim from the immediate area.
- Keep the victim calm. Acute stress reaction increases blood flow and endangers the patient. Keep people near the patient calm. Panic is infectious and compromises judgment.
- Call for help to arrange for transport to the nearest hospital emergency room, where antivenom for snakes common to the area will often be available.
- Make sure to keep the bitten limb in a functional position and below the victim's heart level so as to minimize blood returning to the heart and other organs of the body.
- Do not give the patient anything to eat or drink. This is especially important with consumable alcohol, a known vasodilator which will speed up the absorption of venom.

Do not administer stimulants or pain medications to the victim, unless specifically directed to do so by a physician.

- Remove any items or clothing which may constrict the bitten limb if it swells (rings, bracelets, watches, footwear, etc.)
- Keep the victim as still as possible.
- Do not incise the bitten site.

Many organisations, including the American Medical Association and American Red Cross, recommend washing the bite with soap and water. However, do not attempt to clean the area with any type of chemical. Australian recommendations for snake bite treatment strongly recommend against cleaning the wound. Traces of venom left on the skin/bandages from the strike can be used in combination with a snake bite identification kit to identify the species of snake. This speeds determination of which antivenom to administer in the emergency room.

A Russell's Viper is being 'Milked'. Laboratories Use Extracted Snake Venom to Produce Antivenom, which is Often the Only Effective Treatment for Potentially Fatal Snakebites

In 1979, Australia's National Health and Medical Research Council formally adopted pressure immobilization as the preferred method of first aid treatment for snakebites in Australia. As of 2009, clinical evidence for pressure immobilization remains limited, with current evidence based almost entirely on anecdotal case reports. This has led most international authorities to question its efficacy.

Despite this, all reputable first aid organisations in Australia recommend pressure immobilization treatment; however, it is not widely adhered to, with one study showing that only a third of snakebite patients attempt pressure immobilization.

Pressure immobilization is not appropriate for cytotoxic bites such as those inflicted by most vipers, but may be effective against neurotoxic venoms such as those of most elapids.

Developed by medical researcher Struan Sutherland in 1978, the object of pressure immobilization is to contain venom within a bitten limb and prevent it from moving through the lymphatic system to the vital organs.

This therapy has two components: pressure to prevent lymphatic drainage, and immobilization of the bitten limb to prevent the pumping action of the skeletal muscles.

Pressure is preferably applied with an elastic bandage, but any cloth will do in an emergency. Bandaging begins two to four inches above the bite (i.e. between the bite and the heart), winding around in overlapping turns and moving up towards the heart, then back down over the bite and past it towards the hand or foot. Then the limb must be held immobile: not used, and if possible held with a splint or sling.

The bandage should be about as tight as when strapping a sprained ankle. It must *not* cut off blood flow, or even be uncomfortable; if it is uncomfortable, the patient will unconsciously flex the limb, defeating the immobilization portion of the therapy.

The location of the bite should be clearly marked on the outside of the bandages. Some peripheral edema is an expected consequence of this process.

Apply pressure immobilization as quickly as possible; if you wait until symptoms become noticeable you will have missed the best time for treatment. Once a pressure bandage has been applied, it should *not* be removed until the patient has reached a medical professional.

The combination of pressure and immobilization may contain venom so effectively that no symptoms are visible for more than 24 hours, giving the illusion of a dry bite. But this is only a delay; removing the bandage releases that venom into the patient's system with rapid and possibly fatal consequences.

Antivenom

Until the advent of antivenom, bites from some species of snake were almost universally fatal. Despite huge advances in emergency therapy, antivenom is often still the only effective treatment for envenomation.

The first antivenom was developed in 1895 by French physician Albert Calmette for the treatment of Indian cobra bites. Antivenom is made by injecting a small amount of venom into an animal (usually a horse or sheep) to initiate an immune system response. The resulting antibodies are then harvested from the animal's blood.

Antivenom is injected into the patient intravenously, and works by binding to and neutralizing venom enzymes. It cannot undo damage already caused by venom, so antivenom treatment should be sought as soon as possible.

Modern antivenoms are usually polyvalent, making them effective against the venom of numerous snake species. Pharmaceutical companies which produce antivenom target their products against the species native to a particular area. Although some people may develop serious adverse reactions to antivenom, such as anaphylaxis, in emergency situations this is usually treatable and hence the benefit outweighs the potential consequences of not using antivenom.

The following treatments have all been recommended at one time or another, but are now considered to be ineffective or outright dangerous. Many cases in which such treatments appear to work are in fact the result of dry bites.

Application of a tourniquet to the bitten limb is generally not recommended. There is no convincing evidence that it is an effective first aid tool as ordinarily applied.

Tourniquets have been found to be completely ineffective in the treatment of *Crotalus durissus* bites, but some positive results have been seen with properly applied tourniquets for cobra venom in the Philippines. Uninformed tourniquet use is dangerous, since reducing or cutting off circulation can lead to gangrene, which can be fatal. The use of a compression bandage is generally as effective, and much safer.

Cutting open the bitten area, an action often taken prior to suction, is not recommended since it causes further damage and increases the risk of infection.

Sucking out venom, either by mouth or with a pump, does not work and may harm the affected area directly. Suction started after 3 minutes removes a clinically insignificant quantity—less than one thousandth of the venom injected—as shown in a human study. In a study with pigs, suction not only caused no improvement but led to necrosis in the suctioned area. Suctioning by mouth presents a risk of further poisoning through the mouth's mucous tissues. The well-meaning family member or friend may also release bacteria into the victim's wound, leading to infection.

Immersion in warm water or sour milk, followed by the application of snake-stones (also known as *la Pierre Noire*), which are believed to draw off the poison in much the way a sponge soaks up water.

- Application of potassium permanganate.
- Use of electroshock therapy. Although still advocated by some, animal testing has shown this treatment to be useless and potentially dangerous.

In extreme cases, where the victims were in remote areas, all of these misguided attempts at treatment have resulted in injuries far worse than an otherwise mild to moderate snakebite. In worst case scenarios, thoroughly constricting tourniquets have been applied to bitten limbs, completely shutting off blood flow to the area. By the time the victims finally reached appropriate medical facilities their limbs had to be amputated.

Most snakebites are caused by non-venomous snakes. Of the roughly 3,000 known species of snake found worldwide, only 15 per cent are considered dangerous to humans. Snakes are found on every continent except Antarctica.

The most diverse and widely distributed snake family, the colubrids, has approximately 700 venomous species, but only five genera—boomslangs, twig snakes, keelback snakes, green snakes, and slender snakes—have caused human fatalities.

Since reporting is not mandatory in many regions of the world, snakebites often go unreported. Consequently, no accurate study has ever been conducted to determine the frequency of snakebites on the international level. However, some estimates put the number at 5.4 million snakebites, 2.5 million envenomings, resulting in perhaps 125,000 deaths. Others estimate 1.2 to 5.5 million snakebites, 421,000 to 1.8 million envenomings, and 20,000 to 94,000 deaths. Many people who survive bites nevertheless suffer from permanent tissue damage caused by venom, leading to disability.

Most snake envenomings and fatalities occur in South Asia, Southeast Asia, and sub-Saharan Africa, with India reporting the most snakebite deaths of any country. In India almost all of these deaths are caused by the Big Four, consisting of the Russell's viper, Indian cobra, saw-scaled viper, and the common krait.

In Burma 80 percent of the approximately 1000 deaths each year from snake bite are caused by the Russell's Viper. Tea plantations sometimes are associated with some elapids such as the common cobras and the king cobra.

In the Neotropics, the lance-headed vipers inflict the majority of fatal bites, although of the many known species, only two, the common lancehead and terciopelo, are responsible for most cases. The tropical rattlesnake is another important species.

In Africa, the puff adder is responsible for most fatalities, although there are regional differences, with the saw-scaled viper inflicting more bites in Northern Africa, where the puff adder is not normally found. Most bites occur in industrial plantations, which attract many types of snake prey.

Banana plantations are associated with vipers such as night adders, while rubber and palm tree plantations attract elapids, including cobras and black mambas. There are also highly venomous colubrids in Africa, such as the boomslang.

In the Middle East, the snakes responsible for most bites tend to be more venomous than European species, but deaths are rare, with some estimating perhaps 100 fatal bites annually.

The coastal viper, Palestine viper, and Lebetine viper are the species involved in most bites. Larger and more venomous elapids, such as the Egyptian cobra, can also be found throughout the Middle East.

In Europe, nearly all of the snakes responsible for venomous bites belong to the viper family, and of these, the nose-horned viper, asp viper, and Lataste's viper inflict the majority of bites. Although Europe has a population of some 731 million people, snake bites only kill about 30 people each year, largely due to wide access to health care services and antivenom, as well as the relatively mild potency of many native species' venom.

In Australia, the only continent where venomous snakes constitute the majority of species, the Taipan, tiger snake and Eastern brown snake inflict virtually all reported venomous bites, with the latter responsible for perhaps 60 per cent of deaths caused by snakebite. Although Australian snakes are highly venomous, wide access to antivenom has made deaths exceedingly rare, with only a few fatalities each year.

Most of the Pacific Islands are free of terrestrial snakes; however, sea snakes are common in the Indian Ocean and tropical Pacific Ocean, but are not found in the Atlantic Ocean or the Caribbean, Mediterranean or Red Seas. While the majority of species live close to shorelines or coral reefs, the yellow-bellied sea snake can be found in the open ocean. Over 50 per cent of bites inflicted by sea snakes, which are generally not aggressive, occur when fishermen attempt to remove snakes which have become tangled in fishing nets.

Symptoms may appear in as little as five minutes or take eight hours to develop, depending on the species and region of the body bitten. Although sea snakes are highly venomous, about 80 per cent of reported bites end up being dry. The advent of antivenom and advances in emergency medicine have reduced fatalities to about 3 per cent of snakebite cases.

Of the 120 known indigenous snake species in North America, only 20 are venomous to human beings, all belonging to the families Viperidae and Elapidae. However, in the United States, every state except Maine, Alaska, and Hawaii is home to at least one of 20 venomous snake species. Most snakebite related deaths in the United States are attributed to Eastern and Western diamondback rattlesnake bites. Further, the majority of bites in the United States occur in the southwestern part of the country, in part because rattlesnake populations in the eastern states are much lower. The state of North Carolina has the highest frequency of reported snakebites, averaging approximately 19 bites per 100,000 persons. The national average is roughly 4 bites per 100,000 persons.

Worldwide, snakebites occur most frequently in the summer season when snakes are active and humans are outdoors. Agricultural and tropical regions report more snakebites than anywhere else. Victims are typically male and between 17 and 27 years of age. Children and the elderly are the most likely to die.

Snakes were both revered and worshipped and feared by early civilizations. The ancient Egyptians recorded prescribed treatments for snakebites as early as the Thirteenth dynasty in the Brooklyn Papyrus, which includes at least seven venomous species common to the region today, such as the horned vipers.

In Judaism, the Nehushtan was a pole with a snake made of copper wrapped around it, similar in appearance to the Rod of Asclepius. The object was considered sacred with the power to heal bites caused by the snakes which had infested the desert, with victims merely having to touch it in order to save themselves from imminent death.

Historically, snakebites were seen as a means of execution in some cultures. In medieval Europe, a form of capital punishment was to throw people into snake pits, leaving victims to die from multiple venomous bites. A similar form of punishment was common in Southern Han during China's Five Dynasties and Ten Kingdoms Period and in India. Snakebites were also used as a form of suicide, most notably by Egyptian queen Cleopatra VII, who reportedly died from the bite of an asp—likely an Egyptian cobra —after hearing of Mark Antony's death.

Snakebite as a surreptitious form of murder has been featured in stories such as Sir Arthur Conan Doyle's *The Adventure of the Speckled Band*, but actual occurrences are virtually unheard of, with only a few documented cases. It has been suggested that Boris III of Bulgaria, who was allied to Nazi Germany during World War II, may have been killed with snake venom, although there is no definitive evidence. At least one attempted suicide by snakebite has been documented in medical literature involving a puff adder bite to the hand.

12 List of Snakes

This is a list of snakes by family, subfamily and genus, mostly according to the continuing work of Dr. Roy W. McDiarmid, available through ITIS. The one exception is the family Colubridae because ITIS information for it is currently incomplete. In this case, taxonomic data from the New Reptile Database was used instead , combined with some information for authorities, years and common names from ITIS.

Suborder: Serpentes - Linnaeus, 1758

Infraorder Alethinophidia Nopcsa, 1923

Family:	Acrochordidae Bonaparte, 1831 – Wart snakes
Genus:	*Acrochordus* Hornstedt, 1787 – Java wart snakes
Family:	Aniliidae Stejneger, 1907 – False coral snakes
Genus:	*Anilius* Oken, 1816 – Pipe snakes
Family:	Anomochilidae Cundall, Wallach & Rossman, 1993 – Deadly snake
Genus:	*Anomochilus* Berg, 1901 – Dwarf pipesnakes
Family:	Atractaspididae Günther, 1858 – Stiletto snakes – taxa
Genus:	*Amblyodipsas* Peters, 1857
Genus:	*Aparallactus* A. Smith, 1849
Genus:	*Atractaspis* A. Smith, 1849 – Stiletto snakes
Genus:	*Brachyophis* Mocquard, 1888
Genus:	*Chilorhinophis* Werner, 1907
Genus:	*Elapotinus* Jan, 1862

Genus:	*Hypoptophis* Boulenger, 1896
Genus:	*Macrelaps* Boulenger, 1896
Genus:	*Micrelaps* Boettger, 1880
Genus:	*Poecilopholis* Boulenger, 1903
Genus:	*Polemon* Jan, 1858
Genus:	*Xenocalamus* Günther, 1868
Family:	Boidae Gray, 1825 – Boas
Subfamily:	Boinae Gray, 1825 – Boas – taxa
Genus:	*Boa* Linnaeus, 1758 – Boas
Genus:	*Candoia* Gray, 1842 – Bevel-nosed boas
Genus:	*Corallus* Daudin, 1803 – Neotropical tree boas
Genus:	*Epicrates* Wagler, 1830 – West Indian boas
Genus:	*Eunectes* Wagler, 1830 – Anacondas
Subfamily:	Erycinae Bonaparte, 1831 – Old World sand boas – taxa
Genus:	*Charina* Gray, 1849 – Rosy boas, rubber boas
Genus:	*Eryx* Daudin, 1803 – Old World sand boas
Genus:	*Gongylophis* Wagler, 1830
Family:	Bolyeriidae Hoffstetter, 1946 – Mauritius snakes
Genus:	*Bolyeria* Gray, 1842
Genus:	*Casarea* Gray, 1842
Family:	Colubridae Oppel, 1811 – Typical snakes
Genus:	*Blythia* Theobold, 1868
Genus:	*Cercaspis*
Genus:	*Cyclocorus*
Genus:	*Elapoidis* F. Boie, 1827
Genus:	*Gongylosoma*
Genus:	*Haplocercus* Günther, 1858
Genus:	*Helophis*
Genus:	*Myersophis*
Genus:	*Oreocalamus*
Genus:	*Poecilopholis*
Genus:	*Rhabdops* Boulenger, 1893

Genus: *Tetralepis* Boettger, 1892
Genus: *Thermophis*
Genus: *Trachischium* Günther, 1853
Subfamily: Xenodermatinae
Genus: *Achalinus*
Genus: *Fimbrios*
Genus: *Oxyrhabdium* Boulenger, 1893
Genus: *Stoliczkaia*
Genus: *Xenodermus*
Genus: *Xylophis* Beddome, 1878
Genus: *Pareatinae*
Genus: *Aplopeltura*
Genus: *Asthenodipsas*
Genus: *Pareas*
Genus: *Calamariinae*
Genus: *Calamaria*
Genus: *Calamorhabdium*
Genus: *Collorhabdium*
Genus: *Etheridgeum*
Genus: *Macrocalamus*
Genus: *Pseudorabdion*
Genus: *Rabdion*
Subfamily: Homalopsinae
Genus: *Bitia* Gray, 1842
Genus: *Cantoria* Girard, 1857
Genus: *Cerberus* Cuvier, 1829 – Dog-faced water snakes
Genus: *Enhydris* Sonnini & Latreille, 1802
Genus: *Erpeton* Lacépède, 1800
Genus: *Fordonia* Gray, 1837
Genus: *Gerarda* Gray, 1849
Genus: *Heurnia* Jong, 1926
Genus: *Homalopsis* Kuhl & Hasselt, 1822
Genus: *Myron* Gray, 1849

Subfamily: Homalopsinae *incertae sedis*
Genus: *Brachyorrhos* Kuhl, 1826
Subfamily: Boodontinae
Genus: *Bothrolycus*
Genus: *Bothrophthalmus*
Genus: *Chamaelycus*
Genus: *Dendrolycus*
Genus: *Dipsina*
Genus: *Dromophis*
Genus: *Gonionotophis*
Genus: *Grayia*
Genus: *Hormonotus*
Genus: *Lamprophis*
Genus: *Lycodonomorphus*
Genus: *Lycophidion*
Genus: *Macroprotodon*
Genus: *Mehelya*
Genus: *Pseudaspis*
Genus: *Pseudoboodon*
Genus: *Pythonodipsas*
Genus: *Scaphiophis*
Subfamily: Boodontinae *incertae sedis*
Genus: *Buhoma*
Genus: *Duberria*
Genus: *Montaspis*
Subfamily: Pseudoxyrhophiinae
Genus: *Alluaudina*
Genus: *Compsophis*
Genus: *Ditypophis*
Genus: *Dromicodryas*
Genus: *Exallodontophis*
Genus: *Geodipsas*
Genus: *Heteroliodon*

Genus: *Ithycyphus*
Genus: *Langaha*
Genus: *Leioheterodon*
Genus: *Liophidium*
Genus: *Liopholidophis*
Genus: *Lycodryas*
Genus: *Madagascarophis*
Genus: *Micropisthodon*
Genus: *Pararhadinaea*
Genus: *Pseudoxyrhopus*
Genus: *Stenophis*
Subfamily: Colubrinae
Genus: *Aeluroglena*
Genus: *Ahaetulla*
Genus: *Argyrogena*
Genus: *Arizona* Kennicott *in* Baird, 1859 – Glossy snakes
Genus: *Bogertophis* Dowling & Price, 1988 – Desert rat snakes
Genus: *Boiga* Fitzinger, 1826 – Boigas, catsnakes
Genus: *Cemophora* Cope, 1860 – Scarlet snakes
Genus: *Chilomeniscus* Cope, 1860 – Sand snakes
Genus: *Chionactis* Cope, 1860 – Shovel-nosed snakes
Genus: *Chironius*
Genus: *Chrysopelea*
Genus: *Coluber* Linnaeus, 1758 – Racers
Genus: *Conopsis* Günther, 1858
Genus: *Coronella*
Genus: *Crotaphopeltis*
Genus: *Cryptophidion*
Genus: *Cyclophiops*
Genus: *Dasypeltis*
Genus: *Dendrelaphis* Boulenger, 1890 – Asian tree snakes
Genus: *Dendrophidion* Fitzinger, 1843

Genus: *Dinodon*
Genus: *Dipsadoboa*
Genus: *Dispholidus*
Genus: *Dolichophis*
Genus: *Dryadophis* Stuart, 1938
Genus: *Drymarchon* Fitzinger, 1843 – Indigo snakes
Genus: *Drymobius* Fitzinger, 1843 – Neotropical racers
Genus: *Drymoluber*
Genus: *Dryocalamus*
Genus: *Dryophiops*
Genus: *Eirenis*
Genus: *Elachistodon*
Genus: *Elaphe* Fitzinger *in* Wagler, 1833 – Rat snakes
Genus: *Ficimia* Gray, 1849 – Mexican hook-nosed snakes
Genus: *Gastropyxis*
Genus: *Geagras* Cope, 1876
Genus: *Gonyophis*
Genus: *Gonyosoma*
Genus: *Gyalopion* Cope, 1860 – Hook-nosed snakes
Genus: *Hapsidophrys*
Genus: *Hemerophis*
Genus: *Hemorrhois*
Genus: *Hierophis*
Genus: *Lampropeltis* Fitzinger, 1843 – Kingsnakes
Genus: *Leptodrymus*
Genus: *Leptophis* Bell, 1825
Genus: *Lepturophis*
Genus: *Liopeltis*
Genus: *Lycodon* Boie, 1826
Genus: *Lycognathophis* Boulenger, 1893
Genus: *Lytorhynchus*
Genus: *Masticophis* Baird & Girard, 1853 – Racers
Genus: *Mastigodryas* Amaral, 1935

Genus: *Meizodon*
Genus: *Oligodon*
Genus: *Opheodrys* Fitzinger, 1843 – Green snakes
Genus: *Oxybelis* Wagler, 1830 – Vine snakes
Genus: *Philothamnus*
Genus: *Phyllorhynchus* Stejneger, 1890 – Leaf-nosed snakes
Genus: *Pituophis* Holbrook, 1842 – Bullsnakes
Genus: *Platyceps*
Genus: *Prosymna*
Genus: *Pseudocyclophis*
Genus: *Pseudoficimia* Bocourt, 1883
Genus: *Pseustes* Fitzinger, 1843
Genus: *Ptyas*
Genus: *Rhamnophis*
Genus: *Rhinobothryum* Wagler, 1830
Genus: *Rhinocheilus* Baird & Girard, 1853 – Long-nosed snakes
Genus: *Rhynchocalamus*
Genus: *Rhynchophis*
Genus: *Salvadora* Baird & Girard, 1853 – Patch-nosed snakes
Genus: *Scaphiodontophis* Taylor & Smith, 1943
Genus: *Scolecophis*
Genus: *Senticolis* Dowling & Fries, 1987 – Green ratsnakes
Genus: *Sibynophis*
Genus: *Simophis* Peters, 1860
Genus: *Sonora* Baird & Girard, 1853 – North American ground snakes
Genus: *Spalerosophis*
Genus: *Spilotes* Wagler, 1830
Genus: *Stegonotus*
Genus: *Stenorrhina* Duméril, 1853

Genus: *Stilosoma* Brown, 1890 – Short-tailed snakes
Genus: *Symphimus* Cope, 1870
Genus: *Sympholis* Cope, 1862
Genus: *Tantilla* Baird & Girard, 1853 – Black-headed snakes
Genus: *Tantillita* Smith, 1941
Genus: *Telescopus*
Genus: *Thelotornis*
Genus: *Thrasops*
Genus: *Trimorphodon* Cope, 1861 – Lyre snakes
Genus: *Xenelaphis*
Genus: *Xyelodontophis*
Subfamily: Psammophiinae
Genus: *Hemirhagerrhis*
Genus: *Malpolon*
Genus: *Mimophis*
Genus: *Psammophis*
Genus: *Psammophylax*
Genus: *Rhamphiophis*
Subfamily: Natricinae
Genus: *Adelophis* Dugès, 1879
Genus: *Afronatrix* Rossman & Eberle, 1977
Genus: *Amphiesma* Duméril, Bibron & Duméril, 1854
Genus: *Amphiesmoides* Malnate, 1961
Genus: *Anoplohydrus* Werner, 1909
Genus: *Aspidura* Wagler, 1830
Genus: *Atretium* Cope, 1861
Genus: *Balanophis* H.M. Smith, 1938
Genus: *Clonophis* Cope, 1889 – Kirtland's snakes
Genus: *Hologerrhum*
Genus: *Hydrablabes*
Genus: *Hydraethiops* Günther, 1872
Genus: *Iguanognathus* Boulenger, 1898

Genus:	*Macropisthodon* Boulenger, 1893
Genus:	*Natrix* Laurenti, 1768
Genus:	*Nerodia* Baird & Girard, 1853 – North American water snakes
Genus:	*Opisthotropis* Günther, 1872
Genus:	*Parahelicops*
Genus:	*Pararhabdophis* Bourret, 1934
Genus:	*Regina* Baird & Girard, 1853 – Crayfish snakes
Genus:	*Rhabdophis* Fitzinger, 1843
Genus:	*Seminatrix* Cope, 1895 – Swamp snakes
Genus:	*Sinonatrix* Rossman and Eberle, 1977
Genus:	*Storeria* Baird & Girard, 1853 – Brown-bellied snakes
Genus:	*Thamnophis* Fitzinger, 1843 – Garter snakes, ribbon snakes
Genus:	*Tropidoclonion* Cope, 1860 – Lined snakes
Genus:	*Tropidonophis* Jan, 1863
Genus:	*Virginia* Baird & Girard, 1853 – Earth snakes
Subfamily:	Natricinae *incertae sedis*
Genus:	*Amplorhinus*
Genus:	*Limnophis* Günther, 1865
Genus:	*Natriciteres* Loveridge, 1953
Genus:	*Psammodynastes*
Genus:	*Xenochrophis* Günther, 1864
Subfamily:	Pseudoxenodontinae
Genus:	*Plagiopholis*
Genus:	*Pseudoxenodon*
Subfamily:	Dipsadinae
Genus:	*Adelphicos* Jan, 1862
Genus:	*Amastridium* Cope, 1861
Genus:	*Atractus* Wagler, 1828
Genus:	*Chersodromus* Reinhardt, 1860
Genus:	*Coniophanes* Hallowell *in* Cope, 1860 – Black-striped snakes

Genus:	*Cryophis* Bogert & Duellman, 1963
Genus:	*Dipsas* Laurenti, 1768
Genus:	*Eridiphas* Leviton & Tanner, 1960
Genus:	*Geophis* Wagler, 1830
Genus:	*Hypsiglena* Cope, 1860 – Night snakes
Genus:	*Imantodes* Duméril, 1853
Genus:	*Leptodeira* Fitzinger, 1843 – Cat-eyed snakes
Genus:	*Ninia* Baird & Girard, 1853
Genus:	*Pliocercus*
Genus:	*Pseudoleptodeira* Taylor, 1939
Genus:	*Rhadinaea* Cope, 1863 – Woodland snakes
Genus:	*Sibon* Fitzinger, 1826
Genus:	*Sibynomorphus* Fitzinger, 1843
Genus:	*Tretanorhinus* Duméril, Bibron & Duméril, 1854
Genus:	*Trimetopon* Cope, 1885
Genus:	*Tropidodipsas*
Genus:	*Urotheca* Bibron, 1843
Subfamily:	Dipsadinae *incertae sedis*
Genus:	*Carphophis* Gervais, 1843 – Worm snakes
Genus:	*Contia* Baird & Girard, 1853 – Sharp-tailed snakes
Genus:	*Crisantophis* Villa, 1971
Genus:	*Diadophis* Baird & Girard, 1853 – Ring-necked snakes
Genus:	*Diaphorolepis* Jan, 1863
Genus:	*Echinanthera* Cope, 1894
Genus:	*Emmochliophis* Fritts & Smith, 1969
Genus:	*Enuliophis*
Genus:	*Enulius* Cope, 1871
Genus:	*Hydromorphus* Peters, 1859
Genus:	*Nothopsis* Cope, 1871
Genus:	*Rhadinophanes* Myers & Campbell, 1981
Genus:	*Synophis* Peracca, 1896
Genus:	*Taeniophallus*

Genus: *Tantalophis* Duellman, 1958
Genus: *Xenopholis* Peters, 1866
Subfamily: Xenodontinae
Genus: *Alsophis* Fitzinger, 1843 – West Indian Racers
Genus: *Antillophis* Maglio, 1970
Genus: *Apostolepis* Cope, 1862
Genus: *Arrhyton* Günther, 1858 – West Indian garden snakes
Genus: *Boiruna*
Genus: *Clelia* Fitzinger, 1826
Genus: *Conophis* Peters, 1860
Genus: *Darlingtonia* Cochran, 1935
Genus: *Ditaxodon* Hoge, 1958
Genus: *Drepanoides* Dunn, 1928
Genus: *Elapomorphus* Wiegmann, 1843
Genus: *Erythrolamprus* Wagler, 1830 – Coral snake mimics
Genus: *Farancia* Gray, 1842 – Mud snakes
Genus: *Helicops* Wagler, 1830
Genus: *Heterodon* Latreille *in* Sonnini & Latreille, 1801 – North American hog-nosed snakes
Genus: *Hydrodynastes* Fitzinger, 1843
Genus: *Hydrops* Wagler, 1830
Genus: *Hypsirhynchus* Günther, 1858
Genus: *Ialtris* Cope, 1862
Genus: *Liophis* Wagler, 1830
Genus: *Lystrophis* Cope, 1885
Genus: *Manolepis* Cope, 1885
Genus: *Oxyrhopus* Wagler, 1830
Genus: *Phalotris*
Genus: *Philodryas* Wagler, 1830
Genus: *Phimophis* Cope, 1860
Genus: *Pseudablabes* Boulenger, 1896
Genus: *Pseudoboa* Schneider, 1801

Genus: *Pseudoeryx* Fitzinger, 1826
Genus: *Psomophis*
Genus: *Rhachidelus* Boulenger, 1908
Genus: *Saphenophis* Myers, 1972
Genus: *Siphlophis* Fitzinger, 1843
Genus: *Tropidodryas* Fitzinger, 1843
Genus: *Umbrivaga* Roze, 1964
Genus: *Uromacer* Duméril, Bibron & Duméril, 1854
Genus: *Uromacerina* Amaral, 1929
Genus: *Waglerophis* Romano & Hoge, 1973
Genus: *Xenodon* F. Boie, 1827
Genus: *Xenoxybelis*
Tribe: Tachymenini
Genus: *Calamodontophis* Amaral, 1963
Genus: *Gomesophis* Hoge & Mertens, 1959
Genus: *Pseudotomodon* Koslowsky, 1896
Genus: *Ptychophis* Gomes, 1915
Genus: *Tachymenis* Wiegmann, 1835
Genus: *Thamnodynastes* Wagler, 1830
Genus: *Tomodon* Duméril & Bibron, 1853
Subfamily: Xenodontinae *incertae sedis*
Genus: *Cercophis* Fitzinger, 1843
Genus: *Lioheterophis* Amaral, 1935
Genus: *Sordellina* Proctor, 1923
Family: Cylindrophiidae Fitzinger, 1843 – Asian pipe snakes
Genus: *Cylindrophis* Wagler, 1828 – Asian pipe snakes
Family: Elapidae F. Boie, 1827 – Elapids
Genus: *Acalyptophis* Boulenger, 1869
Genus: *Acanthophis* Daudin, 1803
Genus: *Aipysurus* Lacépède, 1804
Genus: *Aspidelaps* Fitzinger, 1843
Genus: *Aspidomorphus* Fitzinger, 1843

Genus: *Astrotia* Fischer, 1855
Genus: *Austrelaps* Worrell, 1963
Genus: *Boulengerina* Dollo, 1886
Genus: *Bungarus* Daudin, 1803
Genus: *Cacophis* Günther, 1863
Genus: *Calliophis* Gray, 1834
Genus: *Demansia* Gray, 1842
Genus: *Dendroaspis* Schlegel, 1848
Genus: *Denisonia* Krefft, 1869
Genus: *Drysdalia* Worrell, 1961
Genus: *Echiopsis* Fitzinger, 1843
Genus: *Elapognathus* Boulenger, 1896
Genus: *Elapsoidea* Bocage, 1866
Genus: *Emydocephalus* Krefft, 1869
Genus: *Enhydrina* Gray, 1849
Genus: *Ephalophis* M.A. Smith, 1931
Genus: *Furina* Duméril, 1853
Genus: *Hemachatus* Fleming, 1822
Genus: *Hemiaspis* Fitzinger, 1861
Genus: *Hemibungarus* Peters, 1862
Genus: *Homoroselaps* Jan, 1858
Genus: *Hoplocephalus* Wagler, 1830
Genus: *Hydrelaps* Boulenger, 1896
Genus: *Hydrophis* Latreille *in* Sonnini & Latreille, 1801
Genus: *Kerilia* Gray, 1849
Genus: *Kolpophis* M.A. Smith, 1926
Genus: *Lapemis* Gray, 1835
Genus: *Laticauda* Laurenti, 1768 – Sea kraits
Genus: *Leptomicrurus* Schmidt, 1937
Genus: *Loveridgelaps* McDowell, 1970
Genus: *Micropechis* Boulenger, 1896
Genus: *Micruroides* Schmidt, 1928 – Sonoran coral snakes
Genus: *Micrurus* Wagler, 1824 – American coral snakes

Genus: *Naja* Laurenti, 1768
Genus: *Notechis* Boulenger, 1896
Genus: *Ogmodon* Peters, 1864
Genus: *Ophiophagus* Günther, 1864
Genus: *Oxyuranus* Kinghorn, 1923
Genus: *Parahydrophis* Burger & Natsuno, 1974
Genus: *Paranaja* Loveridge, 1944
Genus: *Parapistoclamus* Roux, 1934
Genus: *Pelamis* Daudin, 1803 – Yellow-bellied sea snake
Genus: *Praescutata* Wall, 1921
Genus: *Pseudechis* Wagler, 1830
Genus: *Pseudohaje* Günther, 1858
Genus: *Pseudonaja* Günther, 1858
Genus: *Rhinoplocephalus* Müller, 1885
Genus: *Salomonelaps* McDowell, 1970
Genus: *Simoselaps* Jan, 1859
Genus: *Sinomicrurus* Slowinski *et al.*, 2001
Genus: *Suta* Worrell, 1961
Genus: *Thalassophis* P. Schmidt, 1852
Genus: *Toxicocalamus* Boulenger, 1896
Genus: *Tropidechis* Günther, 1863
Genus: *Vermicella* Gray *in* Günther, 1858
Genus: *Walterinnesia* Lataste, 1887
Family: Loxocemidae Cope, 1861 – Mexican burrowing python
Genus: *Loxocemus* Cope, 1861 – Mexican burrowing python
Family: Pythonidae Fitzinger, 1826 – Pythons – taxa, synonyms, common names
Genus: *Antaresia* Wells & Wellington, 1984
Genus: *Apodora* Kluge, 1993
Genus: *Aspidites* Peters, 1877
Genus: *Bothrochilus* Fitzinger, 1843
Genus: *Leiopython* Hubrecht, 1879

Genus: *Liasis* Gray, 1842
Genus: *Morelia* Gray, 1842
Genus: *Python* Daudin, 1803 – Pythons
Family: Tropidophiidae Brongersma, 1951 – Dwarf boas taxa synonyms, common names
Genus: *Exiliboa* Bogert, 1968
Genus: *Trachyboa* Peters, 1860
Genus: *Tropidophis* Bibron in Sagra, 1843 – Dwarf boas
Genus: *Ungaliophis* Müller, 1880
Family: Uropeltidae Müller, 1832 – Shield-tailed snakes – taxa , synonyms, common names
Genus: *Brachyophidium* Wall, 1921
Genus: *Melanophidium* Günther, 1864
Genus: *Platyplectrurus* Günther, 1868
Genus: *Plectrurus* Duméril, 1851
Genus: *Pseudotyphlops* Schlegel, 1839
Genus: *Rhinophis* Hemprich, 1820
Genus: *Teretrurus* Beddome, 1886
Genus: *Uropeltis* Cuvier, 1829
Family: Viperidae Oppel, 1811 – Vipers
Subfamily: Azemiopinae Liem, Marx & Rabb, 1971 – Fae's viper
Genus: *Azemiops* Boulenger, 1888 – Fae's viper
Subfamily: Causinae Cope, 1859 – Night adders – synonyms, common names
Genus: *Causus* Wagler, 1830 – Night adders
Subfamily: Crotalinae Oppel, 1811 – Pitvipers – taxa , synonyms, common names
Genus: *Agkistrodon* Palisot de Beauvois, 1799 – Mocca sins
Genus: *Atropoides* Werman, 1992 – Jumping vipers
Genus: *Bothriechis* Peters, 1859 – Palm vipers
Genus: *Bothriopsis* Peters, 1861 – Forest vipers
Genus: *Bothrops* Wagler, 1824 – Lanceheads – synonyms, common names

Genus:	*Calloselasma* Cope, 1860 – Malayan pit viper
Genus:	*Cerrophidion* Campbell & Lamar, 1992 – Montane pit vipers
Genus:	*Crotalus* Linnaeus, 1758 – Rattlesnakes – synonyms, common names
Genus:	*Deinagkistrodon* Gloyd, 1979 – Hundred-pace viper
Genus:	*Gloydius* Hoge & Romano-Hoge, 1981
Genus:	*Hypnale* Fitzinger, 1843 – Humpnose vipers
Genus:	*Lachesis* Daudin, 1803 – Bushmasters
Genus:	*Ophryacus* Cope, 1887 – Mexican horned pitvipers
Genus:	*Ovophis* Burger, 1981 – Asian mountain pitvipers
Genus:	*Porthidium* Cope, 1871 – Hognose pit vipers
Genus:	*Sistrurus* Garman, 1883 – Ground rattlesnakes
Genus:	*Trimeresurus* Lacépède, 1804 – Asian pitvipers – synonyms, common names
Genus:	*Tropidolaemus* Wagler, 1830 – Temple vipers
Subfamily:	Viperinae Oppel, 1811 – Pitless vipers – taxa, synonyms, common names
Genus:	*Adenorhinos* Marx & Rabb, 1965 – Uzungwe viper
Genus:	*Atheris* Cope, 1862 – Bush vipers
Genus:	*Bitis* Gray, 1842 – Puff adders
Genus:	*Cerastes* Laurenti, 1768 – Horned vipers
Genus:	*Daboia* Gray, 1842 – Russell's viper
Genus:	*Echis* Merrem, 1820 – Saw-scaled vipers, carpet vipers
Genus:	*Eristicophis* Alcock & Finn, 1897 – McMahon's viper
Genus:	*Macrovipera* Reuss, 1927 – Large Palearctic vipers
Genus:	*Montatheris* Broadley, 1996 – Kenya mountain viper
Genus:	*Proatheris* Broadley, 1996 – Lowland viper
Genus:	*Pseudocerastes* Boulenger, 1896 – False horned vipers

Genus: *Vipera* Laurenti, 1768 – Palearctic vipers

Family: Xenopeltidae Bonaparte, 1845 – Sunbeam snakes

Genus: *Xenopeltis* Reinwardt, 1827

Infraorder Scolecophidia Cope, 1864

Family: Anomalepididae Taylor, 1939 – Primitive blind snakes – taxa, synonyms, common names

Genus: *Anomalepis* Jan, 1860

Genus: *Helminthophis* Peters, 1860

Genus: *Liotyphlops* Peters, 1881

Genus: *Typhlophis* Fitzinger, 1843

Family: Leptotyphlopidae Stejneger, 1892 – Deadly snake – taxa, synonyms, common names

Genus: *Leptotyphlops* Fitzinger, 1843 – Slender blind snakes

Genus: *Rhinoleptus* Orejas-Miranda, Roux-Estève & Guibé, 1970

Family: Typhlopidae Merrem, 1820 – Typical blind snakes – taxa, synonyms, common names

Genus: *Acutotyphlops* Wallach, 1995

Genus: *Cyclotyphlops* Bosch and Ineich, 1994

Genus: *Ramphotyphlops* Fitzinger, 1843 – Long-tailed blind snakes

Genus: *Rhinotyphlops* Fitzinger, 1843

Genus: *Typhlops* Oppel, 1811 – Blind snakes – synonyms, common names

Genus: *Xenotyphlops* Wallach & Ineich, 1996

Boomslang

Corn Snake

Cobra [*Naja naja*]

Red-tailed Green Ratsnake (*Gonyosoma Oxycephalum*)

Timber Rattlesnake (*Crotalus horridus*) with Clearly Visible Facial Pits

Two Male Northern Pacific Rattlenakes (*Crotalus oreganus oreganus*) Engage in a Combat Dance

Agkistrodon contortrix

Broad-banded Copperhead

King Cobra

A Baby King Cobra

Eastern Coral Snake, *Micrurus fulvius*

Crotalus Cerastes

Eye Scales Visible During the Moult of a Diamond Python

An Indian Cobra in a Basket with a Snake Charmer. These Snakes are Perhaps the most Common Subjects of Snake Charmings

Rainbow Boas get Their Name from the Colouration of Their Scales caused by Iridescence

Elaborately Shaped Scales on the Head of a Vine Snake, *Ahaetulla nasuta*

13 Snake Skeleton

A snake skeleton consists primarily of the skull, vertebrae, and ribs, with only vestigial remnants of the limbs.

The skull of a snake is a very complex structure, with numerous joints to allow the snake to swallow prey far larger than its head.

The typical snake skull has a solidly ossified braincase, with the separate frontal bones and the united parietal bones extending downward to the basisphenoid, which is large and extends forward into a rostrum extending to the ethmoidal region. The nose is less ossified, and the paired nasal bones are often attached only at their base. The occipital condyle is either trilobate and formed by the basioccipital and the exoccipitals, or a simple knob formed by the basioccipital; the supraoccipital is excluded from the foramen magnum. The basioccipital may bear a strong, curved ventral process or hypapophysis in the vipers.

The prefrontal bone is situated, on each side, between the frontal bone and the maxilla, and may or may not be in contact with the nasal bone.

The postfrontal bone, usually present, borders the orbit behind, rarely also above, and in the pythons a supraorbital bone is intercalated between it and the prefrontal bone.

The premaxillary bone is single and small, and as a rule connected with the maxillary only by ligament.

The paired vomer is narrow.

The palatine bone and pterygoid are long and parallel to the axis of the skull, the latter diverging behind and extending to the quadrate or to the articular extremity of the mandible; the pterygoid is connected with the maxillary by the ectopterygoid or transverse bone, which may be very long, and the maxillary often emits a process towards the palatine, the latter bone being usually produced inwards and upwards towards the anterior extremity of the basisphenoid.

The quadrate is usually large and elongate, and attached to the cranium through the supratemporal (often regarded as the squamosal).

In rare cases (Miodon, Polemon) the transverse bone is forked, and articulates with two branches of the maxilla.

The quadrate and the maxillary and palatopterygoid arches are more or less movable to allow for the distension required by the passage of prey, often much exceeding the size of the mouth. For the same reason, the rami of the lower jaw, which consist of dentary, splenial, angular, and articular elements, with the addition of a coronoid in the boas and a few other small families, are connected at the symphysis by a very extensible elastic ligament.

The hyoid apparatus is reduced to a pair of cartilaginous filaments situated below the trachea, and united in front.

There are various modifications according to the genera. A large hole may be present between the frontal bones and the basisphenoid (Psammophis, Coelopeltis); the maxillary may be much abbreviated and movable vertically, as in the Viperidae; the pterygoids may taper and converge posteriorly, without any connection with the quadrate, as in the Amblycephalidae; the supratemporal may be much reduced, and wedged in between the adjacent bones of the cranium; the quadrate may be short or extremely large; the prefrontals may join in a median suture in front of the frontals; the dentary may be freely movable, and detached from the articular posteriorly.

The deviation from the normal type is much greater still when we consider the degraded wormlike members of the families Typhlopidae and Glauconiidae, in which the skull is very compact and the maxillary much reduced. In the former this bone is loosely attached to the lower aspect of the cranium; in the latter it borders the mouth, and is suturally joined to the premaxillary and the prefrontal. In both the transverse bone and the supratemporal are absent, but the coronoid element is present in the mandible.

Joints of the Snake Skull

Lateral view of the skull of a Burmese python, with visible kinetic joints labeled. Red = highly mobile, green = slightly mobile, blue = immobile.

Red A: The joint between the mandible and quadrate. It is analogous to the joint in mammal jaws.

Red B: The joint between the quadrate and the supratemporal. It is highly mobile in most directions, allowing a wider gape (i.e., the snake can open its mouth wider) and greater jaw flexibility.

Red C: The joint between the prefrontal and maxilla. It allows the maxilla to pivot in the plane of the photograph, and while it does not increase gape, it does facilitate the complex action by which the snake draws prey into its mouth.

Green A: The joint between the frontal bone and nasal bone. It allows the nose to upturn slightly, increasing gape and assisting in swallowing.

Green B: Allows the lower jaws to bow outwards, further increasing the gape.

Blue: The joint between the supratemporal and parietal. Immobile, except for Dasypeltis.

Snake Dentition

In most snakes, teeth are located on the dentary of the lower jaw, the maxilla, the palatine bone and the lateral pterygoid plate. The latter form an 'inner row' of teeth that can move separately from the rest of the jaws and are used to help 'walk' the jaws over prey. While most snakes are not hazardous to humans, several lineages have evolved venom which is typically delivered by specialized teeth called fangs located on the maxilla.

Most snakes can be placed into one of four groups, based on their teeth, which correlate strongly with venom and lineage.

Aglyphous snakes (*lacking grooves*) have no specialized teeth; each tooth is similar in shape and often size. When teeth vary in size, as in some bird eaters, they do not vary in shape. Most aglyphous snakes are non-venomous, however some, like Thamnophis, are considered mildly venomous, but generally not harmful to humans. The feature is not a synapomorphy.

Proteroglyphous snakes (*forward grooved*) have shortened maxillae bearing few teeth except for a substantially enlarged fang pointing downwards and completely folded around the venom channel, forming a hollow needle. Because the fangs are only a fraction of an inch long in even the largest species these snakes must hang on, at least momentarily, as they inject their venom, the most toxic of all snakes. Some spitting cobras have modified fang tips allowing them to spray venom at an attacker's eyes. This form of dentition is unique to elapids.

Solenoglyphous snakes (*pipe grooved*) have the most advanced venom delivery method of any snake. Each maxilla is reduced to a nub supporting a single hollow fang tooth. The fangs, which can be as long as half the length of the head, are folded against the roof of the mouth, pointing posteriorly.

The skull has a series of interacting elements which ensure that the fangs rotate into biting position when the jaws open. Solenoglyphous snakes open their mouths almost 180 degrees, and the fangs swing into a position to allow them to penetrate deep into the prey. While solenoglyph venom is typically less toxic than that of proteroglyphs, this system allows them to deeply inject large quantities of venom. This form of dentition is unique to vipers.

A few snakes do not conform to these categories. Atractaspis is solenoglyphous but the fangs swing out sideways, allowing it to strike without opening its mouth, perhaps allowing it to hunt in small tunnels. Scolecophidia (blind burrowing snakes) typically have few teeth, often only in the upper jaw or lower jaw.

Taxonomic Key of Skull Modifications

Modifications of the skull in the European genera:

1. Quadrate articulating with the cranium, supratemporal absent; mandible much shorter than the skull, with coronoid bone; maxillary small, on lower aspect of cranium; pterygoids not extending to quadrate; nasals forming long sutures with the premaxillary, prefrontals, and frontal: *Typhlops*.
2. Quadrate suspended from the supratemporal; mandible at least as long as the skull; pterygoids extending to quadrate or mandible.
3. Mandible with coronoid bone; nasals in sutural contact with frontals and prefrontals; transverse bone short, not projecting much beyond cranium; maxillary not half as long as mandible, which is not longer than skull (to occiput): *Eryx*.
4. No coronoid bone; nasals isolated
5. Maxillary elongate, not movable vertically.
6. Maxillary half as long as mandible.
   (a) Supratemporal half as long as skull, projecting far beyond cranium; mandible much longer than skull: *Tropidonotus*.
   (b) Supratemporal not half as long as skull, projecting far beyond cranium; mandible much longer than skull: *Zamenis*.
   (c) Supratemporal not half as long as skull, projecting but slightly beyond cranium; mandible much longer than skull: *Coluber*.
   (d) Supratemporal not half as long as skull, not projecting beyond cranium; mandible not longer than skull: *Coronella, Contia*.

7. Maxillary not half as long as mandible, which is longer than skull; supratemporal not half as long as skull, projecting beyond cranium.
   (*a*) Quadrate longer than supratemporal; maxillary much longer than quadrate, nearly straight in front of prefrontal; a large vacuity between the frontal bones and the basisphenoid: *Coelopeltis*.
   (*b*) Quadrate not longer than supratemporal; maxillary little longer than quadrate, strongly curved in front of prefrontal: *Macroprotodon*.
   (*c*) Quadrate longer than supratemporal; maxillary little longer than quadrate, nearly straight in front of prefrontal: *Tarbophis*.
8. Maxillary much abbreviated and erectile; supratemporal not half as long as skull; mandible much longer than skull; basioccipital with a strong process.
   (*a*) Maxillary bone solid: *Vipera*.
   (*b*) Maxillary bone hollow: *Ancistrodon*.
   (*c*) The vertebrae number 130 to 500 - in the European forms 147 (*Vipera ursinii*) to 330 (*Coluber leopardinus*).

Vertebrae and Ribs

The vertebral column consists of an atlas (composed of two vertebrae) without ribs; numerous precaudal vertebrae, all of which, except the first or first three, bear long, movable, curved ribs with a small posterior tubercle at the base, the last of these ribs sometimes forked; two to ten so-called lumbar vertebrae without ribs, but with bifurcate transverse processes (lymphapophyses) enclosing the lymphatic vessels; and a number of ribless caudal vertebrae with simple transverse processes. When bifid, the ribs or transverse processes have the branches regularly superposed.

The centra have the usual ball and socket joint, with the nearly hemispherical or transversely elliptic condyle at the back (procoelous vertebrae), while the neural arch is provided with additional articular surfaces in the form of pre- and post-zygapophyses, broad, flattened, and overlapping, and of a pair of anterior wedge-shaped processes called zygosphene, fitting into a pair of corresponding concavities, zygantrum, just below the base of the neural spine. Thus the vertebrae of snakes articulate with each other by eight joints in addition to the cup-and-ball on the centrum, and interlock by parts reciprocally receiving and entering one another, like the mortise and tenon jointery.

The precaudal vertebrae have a more or less high neural spine which, as a rare exception (Xenopholis), may be expanded and plate-like above, and short or moderately long transverse processes to which the ribs are attached by a single facet. The centra of the anterior vertebrae emit more or less developed descending processes, or haemapophyses, which are sometimes continued throughout, as in Tropidonotus, Vipera, and Ancistrodon, among European genera.

In the caudal region, elongate transverse processes take the place of ribs, and the haemapophyses are paired, one on each side of the haemal canal. In the rattlesnakes the seven or eight last vertebrae are enlarged and fused into one.

Vestigial Limbs

Skeleton of a Boelens python showing the bones inside the anal spurs.

No living snake shows any remains of the pectoral arch, but remains of the pelvis are found in:

- *Boas and Pythons:* A long ilium, attached to the lower branch of the first bifurcate transverse process of the lumbar vertebrae, bearing three short bones, the longest of which, regarded as the femur, terminates in a claw-like pelvic spur which usually appears externally on each side of the cloaca.
- *Leptotyphlopidae:* Ilium, pubis, and ischium, and rudimentary femur, the ischium forming a ventral symphysis.
- Aniliidae.
- *Typhlopidae:* A single bone on each side.

14 Corn Snake

The Corn Snake (*Elaphe guttata*), or Red Rat Snake, is a North American species of Rat Snake that subdues its small prey by constriction. The name 'Corn Snake' is a holdover from the days when southern farmers stored harvested ears of corn in a wood frame or log building called a crib. Rats and mice came to the corn crib to feed on the corn, and Corn Snakes came to feed on the rodents. The *Oxford English Dictionary* cites this usage as far back as 1676. Corn Snakes are found throughout the southeastern and central United States. Their docile nature, reluctance to bite, moderate adult size 3.9-5.9 feet (1.2-1.8 m), attractive pattern, and comparatively simple care make them popular pet snakes. In the wild, they usually live around 6-8 years, but in captivity can live to be up to 23 years old.

There are two subspecies of *Elaphe guttata*:

1. The Corn Snake (*Elaphe guttata guttata*) lives in the southeastern United States, and is distinguished by having brownish-orange skin with orange/red saddles, the saddles having black borders, and usually a black and white underbelly.
2. The Great Plains Rat Snake or Emory's Rat Snake (*Elaphe guttata emoryi*) is found in the United States from Nebraska to Texas, and into northern Mexico.

Further taxonomic controversy has included the taxonomic suggestion that the genus be changed to *Pantherophis, Russian Journal of Herpetology* 9(2): 105-124) but this was rejected by Crother et al. in (2003) Update. Herp. Rev. 34: 196-203. The International Committee for Zoological Nomenclature has not endorsed the change to *Pantherophis*, thus the correct genus remains *Elaphe*.

Wild Corn Snakes prefer habitats such as overgrown fields, forest openings, trees, palmetto flatwoods and abandoned or seldom-used buildings and farms, from sea level to as high as 6000 feet. Typically, these snakes remain on the ground, but can ascend trees, cliffs and other elevated surfaces. They can be found in the southeastern United States ranging from New Jersey to the Florida keys and as far west as Texas.

In colder regions, snakes hibernate during winter. However, in the more temperate climate along the coast they shelter in rock crevices and logs during cold weather, and come out on warm days to soak up the heat of the sun, a process known as brumation. During cold weather, snakes are less active and therefore hunt less.

Diet

Corn Snakes have a diet primarily consisting of rodents, mostly mice and rats. Prey is killed by constriction. They are proficient climbers and may scale trees in search of birds and bats although they prefer to be on ground level. As litters of infant mice are difficult to find in nature, many neonate Corn Snakes are known to eat small lizards as their first meals, and anoles are the preferred choice. Some individuals retain these dietary tendencies well into adulthood.

Captive Corn Snakes are usually fed by their owners on a diet of commercially available rodents, predominantly mice, while younger and smaller specimens may eat live or dead rat or mouse pups of various sizes. Frozen mice that have been thawed to room temperature are usually preferred, as live prey can possibly carry disease or injure the snake if it has not been raised on live prey. Corn Snakes usually breed shortly after the winter cooling. The male courts the female primarily with tactile and chemical cues, then everts one of his hemipenes, inserts it into the female, and ejaculates his sperm. If the female is ovulating, the eggs will be fertilized, and she will begin sequestering nutrients into the eggs, then secreting a shell.

Egg-laying occurs slightly more than a month after mating, with 12–24 eggs deposited into a warm, moist, hidden location. Once laid the adult snake abandons the eggs and does not return to them. The eggs are oblong with a leathery, flexible shell. Approximately 10 weeks after laying, the young snakes use a specialized scale called an egg tooth to slice slits in the egg shell, from which they emerge at about 5 inches in length.

After many generations of selective breeding, domesticated Corn Snakes are found in a wide variety of different colours and patterns. These result from recombining the dominant and recessive genes that code for proteins involved in chromatophore development, maintenance, or function. New variations, or morphs, become available every year as breeders gain a better understanding of the genetics involved.

Colour Morphs

Normal or wildtype Corn Snakes are orange with black lines around red coloured saddle markings going down their back with black and white checkered bellies. Regional diversity is found in wild caught Corn Snakes, the most popular being the Miami and Okeetee phases. These are the most commonly seen Corn Snakes.

- *Miami Phase* (originates in the Florida wildtype) These are usually smaller Corn Snakes with some specimens having highly contrasting light silver to gray ground colour with orange saddle markings surrounded in black. Selective breeding has lightened the ground colour and darkened the saddle marks. The 'Miami' name, coined by Rich Zuchowski, now is considered an appearance trait. Many Miami Corn Snakes are difficult to start feeding as hatchlings, as they prefer lizards. Miami Corn Snakes, unlike other varieties, will often readily accept anoles as food for life. This can simplify feeding for residents of Florida, but care should be taken to avoid introducing parasites from wild caught food.

- *Okeetee Corn Snakes* (classic Corn Snakes, originate in the South Carolina wildtype). These snakes are characterized by deep red dorsal saddle marks surrounded by very black borders. The ground colour varies with bright orange being popular amongst breeders. As with the Miami phase, selective breeding has changed the term 'Okeetee' to an appearance rather than a locality. Some on the market originate solely from selectively breeding Corn Snakes from the Okeetee Hunt Club.
- *Candycane* (selectively bred amelanistic) These are amelanistic Corn Snakes bred toward the ideal of red saddle marks on a white background. Some were produced using light creamsicle (emory/albino corn hybrids x corn) bred with Miami phase Corn Snakes. Most candy canes develop orange colouration around the neck region as they mature and many labeled as candycanes later develop significant amounts of yellow or orange in the ground colour. The contrast they have as hatchlings often fades with maturity.
- *Reverse Okeetee* (selectively bred amelanistic) an amelanistic Okeetee Corn Snake which has the normal black rings around the saddle marks replaced with wide white rings. Ideal specimens are high contrast snakes with light orange to yellow background and dark orange/red saddles. *Note:* Albino Okeetees are not locale-specific okeetees—they are selectively bred amelanistics.
- *Fluorescent orange* (selectively bred amelanistic) develop white borders around bright red saddle marks as adults on an orange background.
- *Sunglow* (selectively bred amelanistic) another designer amelanistic corn that lacks the usual white speckling that often appears in most albinos, and selected for exceptionally bright ground colour. The orange background surrounds dark orange saddle marks.

- *Bloodred* (selectively bred 'Diffused') Corn Snakes carry a recessive trait (known as diffused) that eliminates the ventral checkered patterns. These originated from a somewhat unicolour Jacksonville and Gainesville, Florida strain of Corn Snake. Through selective breeding, an almost solid ground colour has been produced. Hatchlings have a visible pattern that can fade as they mature into a solid orange red to ash red coloured snake. The earlier bloodreds tend to have large clutches of smaller than average eggs that produce hard to feed offspring, though out-crossing with amelanistic and anerythristic Corn Snake hatchlings tend to be larger with fewer feeding problems.
- *Crimson* (hypomelanistic + Miami) are very light high contrast snakes with a light background and dark red/ orange saddle marks.
- *Anerythristic* (anerythristic A, Sometimes called black albino) are the complement to amelanism. The inherited recessive mutation of lacking erythrin (red, yellow, and orange) pigments produces a snake that is mostly black, gray and brown. When mature, many type A anerythristic Corn Snakes develop yellow on their neck regions. In 1984 a Type B anerythristic Corn Snake was caught in the wild; it is the ancestor of anerythristics missing the yellow neck regions. Similar snakes include: stonewashed-copper or light brown saddle marks; charcoal (aka muted anerythristic, Pine Island anerythristic); type B anerythristic, very low contrast with shades of gray on white and black background.
- *Charcoal:* These snakes (sometimes known as anerythristic type 'B') can lack the yellow colour pigment usually found in all Corn Snakes. They are a more muted contrast compared to Anerythristics.
- *Caramel:* Corn Snakes are another Rich Zuchowski engineered Corn Snake. The background is varying shades of yellow to yellow-brown. Dorsal saddle marks vary from caramel yellow to brown, and chocolate brown.

- *Lavender:* Corn Snakes contain a light pink background with darker purple gray markings and burgundy eyes or lavender gray saddle marks on an orangish background. Variation with this same genetic strain are arguably called mocha, cocoa, and chocolate.
- *Cinder* reduced red pigment which becomes more like an anerythristic as they become adults.
- *Kastanie:* This gene was first discovered in Germany. Kastanies hatch out looking nearly anerythristic but gain some colour as they mature, to eventually take on a chestnut colouration.
- *Hypomelanistic* or rosy Corn Snakes carry a recessive trait that reduces the dark pigments causing the reds, whites, and oranges to become more vivid. Their eyes remain dark. These snakes range in appearance between amelanistic Corn Snakes to normals with greatly reduced melanin.
- *Ultra:* Ultra is a hypomelanistic-like gene that is an allele to the amelanistic gene. Ultra Corn Snakes have light grey lines in place of black.
- *Ultramel* is an intermediate appearance between ultra and amel which is the result of being heterozygous for ultra and amel at the albino locus.
- *Dilute* is another melanin-reducing gene.
- *Sunkissed* is a hypo-like gene which was first found in Kathy Love's colony.
- *Lava* is an extreme hypo-like gene which was discovered by Joe Pierce and named by Jeff Mohr.
- *Stargazing* is not a colour morph, but a chronic deficiency in balance. It is caused by a simple-recessive genetic defect and is considered deleterious.

Pattern Morphs

- *Motley* a snake with a clear belly and an 'inverted' spotting pattern. May also appear as stripes or dashes.
- *Stripe* this morph also has a clear belly and a striping pattern. Unlike the motley the stripes will not connect,

but may sometimes break up and take on a "cubed" appearance. Cubes and spots on a striped corn are the same as the saddle colour on a similar normal corn, unlike motley snakes. Stripe is both allelic and recessive to motley, so breeding a striped corn and a (homozygous) motley corn will result in all motley Corn Snakes, and breeding these (heterozygous) motley corn offspring will result in ¾ motley and ¼ striped Corn Snakes.

- *Diffusion* diffuses the patterning on the sides and eliminates the belly pattern. It is one component of the bloodred morph.
- *Sunkissed* while considered a hypo-like gene, sunkissed also has other effects such as rounded saddles and unusual head patterns.

Compound Morphs

There are tens of thousands of possible compound morphs. Some of the most popular are listed:

1. *Snow* (Amelanistic + Anerythristic) As hatchlings this colour variation is composed of white and pink blotches. These predominantly white snakes tend to have yellow neck and throat regions when mature. Light blotches and background colours have subtle shades of beige, ivory, pink, green, or yellow.
2. *Blizzard* (Amelanistic + Anerythristic B) Corn Snakes resulted from a type B anerythristic corn caught in 1984. Blizzards are a totally white snake with very little to no visible pattern.
3. *Ghost* (Hypomelanistic + Anerythristic A) Corn Snakes are a hypomelanistic anerythristic (type A) snakes. They exhibit varying shades of grays, browns, and blacks on a lighter background. These often create pastel colours in lavenders, pinks, oranges, and browns.
4. *Phantom:* These are a combination of charcoal and Hypomelanistic.
5. *Pewter* (Charcoal + Diffused) are silvery lavender with very slight blotches as adults.

6. *Butter* (Amelanistic + Caramel) A two-tone yellow Corn Snake with bits of white between markings.
7. *Amber* (Hypomelanistic + Caramel) Corn Snakes are a hypomelanistic caramel snake with amber markings on a brownish background.
8. *Gold Dust* (Ultramel + Caramel) Gold Dust Corn Snakes often have a more golden yellow than butters mixed with the grey lines rather than white.
9. *Plasma* (Diffused + Lavander) Hatch out in varying shade of purple.
10. *Opal* (Amelanistic + Lavender) look like blizzard Corn Snakes once mature with pink to purple highlights.

Intergrades

- *Root Beer* are intergrades between a normal Corn Snake and a Great Plains Rat Snake (Emory's Rat Snake). This morph looks much like a sepia-toned Corn Snake.
- *Creamsicle* are intergrades between an albino Corn Snake and an Emory's Rat Snake/common corn cross. These snakes bring out the yellow and downplay the reds of the Corn Snake. Most are varying shades of yellow with darker yellow to orangish blotches. Clutches are generally smaller in number but produce larger, more vigorous hatchlings. Creamsicle with less emory background and increased amelanistic corn generally have lighter backgrounds and red to orange saddles (red creamsicle).
- *Cinnamon* is the hypomelanistic phase of the Corn Snake × Great Plains Rat Snake

Hybrids

- *Jungle* Corn Snakes are hybrids using the Corn Snake and California Kingsnake (*Lampropeltis getula californiae*). These show extreme pattern variations taking markings from both parents—sometimes looking very similar to one parent or the other. Although they are hybrids of different genera, they are not sterile.

Kingsnake

Kingsnakes are a type of colubrid snake that are members of the *Lampropeltis* genus, which also includes the milk snake along with another four species and 45 sub-species.

Lampropeltis means 'shiny shield', a name given to them in reference to their dorsal scales. The majority of kingsnakes have quite vibrant patterns on their skin. Kingsnakes use constriction to kill their prey and tend to be opportunistic when it comes to their diet; they will eat other snakes (ophiophagy), including venomous snakes, lizards, rodents, birds and eggs. The Common Kingsnake genus are known to be immune to the venom of other snakes and are known to eat rattlesnakes (*Note:* Kingsnakes are not necessarily immune to the venom of snakes from different *localities*). The 'king' in their name (as with the king cobra) references their taste for other snakes.

Some species of kingsnake, such as the Scarlet Kingsnake, have colouration and patterning which can cause them to be confused with the venomous coral snakes. There are mnemonic rhymes to help people distinguish between the coral snake and its non-venomous look-alikes, including "Red and yellow kills a fellow. Red and black is safe for Jack."

Taxonomic reclassification is an ongoing process, and different sources often disagree, granting full species status to a group of these snakes that another source considers a subspecies. In the case of *Lampropeltis catalinensis*, for example, only a single specimen exists, and therefore classification is not necessarily finite. In addition, hybridization between species which have overlapping geographic ranges is not uncommon, confusing taxonomists further.

Kingsnakes are commonly kept as pets, due to their ease of care. Kingsnakes are overall hardy and simple to care for. Their captive diet usually consists of appropriately sized rodents, prekilled. Giving live rodents is an illegal offense in some countries and may be bad for the snake's health, as live rodents are capable of delivering powerful bites, potentially injuring the snake. Kingsnakes are generally docile, curious and gentle.

- Grey-Banded Kingsnake, *Lampropeltis alterna* (Brown, 1901)
- *Lampropeltis calligaster*
- Prairie Kingsnake, *Lampropeltis calligaster* (Harlan, 1827)
- South Florida Mole Kingsnake, *Lampropeltis calligaster occipitolineata* Price, 1987
- Mole Kingsnake, *Lampropeltis calligaster rhombomaculata* (Holbrook, 1840)
- Common Kingsnake, *Lampropeltis getula*
- California Kingsnake, *Lampropeltis getula californiae* (Blainville, 1835)
- Florida Kingsnake, *Lampropeltis getula floridana* (Blanchard, 1919)
- Eastern Kingsnake, *Lampropeltis getula getula* (Linnaeus, 1766)
- Apalachicola Kingsnake, *Lampropeltis getula meansi* (Krysko & Judd, 2006)
- Speckled Kingsnake, *Lampropeltis getula holbrooki* (Stejneger, 1902)
- Black Kingsnake, *Lampropeltis getula niger* (Yarrow, 1882)
- Western Black Kingsnake, *Lampropeltis getula nigrita* (Zweifel & Norris, 1955)
- Desert Kingsnake, *Lampropeltis getula splendida* (Baird & Girard, 1853)
- Isla Santa Catalina Kingsnake Lampropeltis "getula" catalinensis (Van Denburgh & Slevin, 1921)
- *Lampropeltis mexicana*
- *Lampropeltis mexicana leonis* (Günther, 1893)
- Durango Mountain Kingsnake, *Lampropeltis mexicana greeri* Webb, 1961
- Nuevo Leon Kingsnake, *Lampropeltis mexicana thayeri* (Loveridge, 1924)
- *Lampropeltis pyromelana*
- Utah Mountain Kingsnake, *Lampropeltis pyromelana infralabialis* (Tanner, 1953)

- Sonoran Mountain Kingsnake, *Lampropeltis pyromelana knoblochi* Taylor, 1940
- Arizona Mountain Kingsnake, *Lampropeltis pyromelana pyromelana* (Cope, 1866)
- Ruthven's Kingsnake, *Lampropeltis ruthveni* (Blanchard, 1920)
- *Lampropeltis triangulum*
- Scarlet Kingsnake, *Lampropeltis triangulum elapsoides* (Holbrook, 1838)
- *Lampropeltis webbi* (Bryson, Dixon & Lazcano, 2005)
- *Lampropeltis zonata*
- San Pedro Kingsnake, *Lampropeltis zonata agalma* (Van Denburgh & Slevin, 1923)
- Todos Santos Island Kingsnake, *Lampropeltis zonata herrerae* (Van Denburgh & Slevin, 1923)
- Sierra Mountain Kingsnake, *Lampropeltis zonata multicincta* (Yarrow, 1882)
- Coast Mountain Kingsnake, *Lampropeltis zonata multifasciata* (Bocourt, 1886)
- San Bernardino Mountain Kingsnake, *Lampropeltis zonata parvirubra* Zweifel, 1952
- San Diego Mountain Kingsnake, *Lampropeltis zonata pulchra* Zweifel, 1952
- St. Helena Mountain Kingsnake, *Lampropeltis zonata zonata* (Blainville, 1835)

Additionally, Alex Pyron and Burbrink have argued that the short-tailed snake, more familiar as *Stilosoma extenuatum*, be included with *Lampropeltis*.

15 Rat Snake

Rat snakes are medium to large constrictors that can be found through a great portion of the northern hemisphere. They feed primarily on rodents and birds and, with some species exceeding 3 m (10 feet), they can occupy top levels of some food chains. Many species make attractive and docile pets and one, the corn snake, is one of the most popular reptile pets in the world. Other species can be very skittish and sometimes aggressive but bites are seldom serious. As with nearly all colubrids, rat snakes pose no threat to humans. Rat snakes were long thought to be completely nonvenomous, but recent studies have shown that some Old World species do possess small amounts of venom (amounts so small as to be negligible to humans).

Previously, most rat snakes were assigned to the genus *Elaphe* but many have been since renamed following mitochondrial DNA analysis performed in 2002. For the purpose of this article names will be harmonized with the TIGR Database. When searching for information on a particular species of rat snake it might be useful to query the old name, *Elaphe sp.*, as well as the new.

Scientific Classification

Kingdom; Animalia Phylum; Chordata Subphylum; Vertebrata Class; Reptilia Subclass; Diapsida Infraclass; Lepidosauromorpha Superorder; Lepidosauria Order; Squamata Infraorder; Serpentes Family; Colubridae Genus; Various.

Old World

- Philippine rat snake (*Coelognathus erythrurus*) Duméril, Bibron & Duméril 1854
- Yellow rat snake (*Coelognathus flavolineatus*) Schlegel 1837
- Trinket snake (*Coelognathus helena*) Daudin 1803
- Copperhead rat snake (*Coelognathus radiata*) Boie 1827
- Indonesian Rat snake (*Coelognathus subradiata*) Schlegel 1837
- Twin-spotted rat snake (*Elaphe bimaculata*) Schmidt 1925
- King rat snake (*Elaphe carinata*) Günther 1864
- Japanese rat snake (*Elaphe climacophora*) Boie 1826
- David's rat snake (*Elaphe davidi*) Sauvage 1884
- Dione rat snake (*Elaphe dione*) Pallas 1773
- Japanese four-lined rat snake (*Elaphe quadrivirgata*) Boie 1826
- Four-lined snake (*Elaphe quatuorlineata*) Lacepede 1789
- Red-backed rat snake (*Elaphe rufodorsata*) Cantor 1842
- Eastern four-lined snake (*Elaphe sauromates*) Pallas 1811
- Russian rat snake (*Elaphe schrenckii*) Strauch 1873
- Japanese forest rat snake (*Euprepiophis conspicillatus*)
- Mandarin rat snake (*Euprepiophis mandarinus*)
- Celebes black-tailed rat snake (*Gonyosoma jansenii*) Bleeker 1858
- Red-tailed green rat snake (*Gonyosoma oxycephalum*) Boie 1827
- Mountain rat snake (*Oreocryptophis porphyracea*) Cantor 1839
- Cantor's rat snake (*Orthriophis cantoris*) Boulenger 1894
- Hodgson's rat snake (*Orthriophis hodgsoni*) Günther 1860
- 100 Flower rat snake (*Orthriophis moellendorffi*) Boettger 1886
- Beauty Snake (*Orthriophis taeniurus*) Cope 1861
- Keeled rat snake (*Ptyas carinata*) Günther 1858
- (*Ptyas dhumnades*) Cantor 1842

- Sulawesi black racer (*Ptyas dipsas*) Schlegel 1837
- White-bellied rat snake (*Ptyas fusca*) Günther 1858
- Chinese rat snake (*Ptyas korros*) Schlegel 1837
- (*Ptyas luzonensis*) Günther 1873
- Oriental rat snake (*Ptyas mucosus*) Linnaeus 1758
- Green rat snake (*Ptyas nigromarginatus*) Blyth 1854
- Green trinket snake (*Rhadinophis frenatum*) Gray 1853
- Green bush snake (*Rhadinophis prasina*) Blyth 1854
- Rhinoceros Ratsnake (*Rhynchophis boulengeri*) Mocquard 1897
- Transcaucasian rat snake (*Zamenis hohenackeri*) Strauch 1873
- Italian Aesculapian snake (*Zamenis lineatus*) Camerano 1891
- Aesculapian snake (*Zamenis longissimus*) Laurenti 1768
- Persian rat snake (*Zamenis persicus*) Werner 1913
- Leopard snake (*Zamenis situla*) Linnaeus 1758

New World

- Baja California rat snake (*Bogertophis rosaliae*) Mocquard 1899
- Trans Pecos rat snake (*Bogertophis subocularis*) Brown 1901
- Eastern rat snake (*Elaphe alleghaniensis*) Holbrook 1836
- Baird's rat snake (*Elaphe bairdi*) Yarrow 1880
- Great Plains rat snake (*Elaphe emoryi*) Baird & Girard 1853
- Eastern fox snake (*Elaphe gloydi*) Conant 1940
- Corn snake (*Elaphe guttata*) Linnaeus 1766
- Western rat snake (*Elaphe obsoleta*) Say 1823
- Central rat snake (*Elaphe spiloides*) Duméril, Bibron & Duméril 1854
- Western foxsnake (*Elaphe vulpina*) Baird & Girard 1853
- Mexican nightsnake (*Pseudelaphe flavirufus*) Cope 1867
- Green rat snake (*Senticolis triaspis*) Cope 1866

In recent years there has been some taxonomic controversy over the genus of North American rat snakes. Based on mitochondrial DNA, researchers showed that North

American Rat Snakes of the genus *Elaphe* along with closely related genera such as *Pituophis* and *Lampropeltis* form a monophyletic group separate from Old World members of the genus. They therefore suggested the resurrection of the available name *Pantherophis* Fitzinger for all North American taxa (north of Mexico).

All published taxonomy remains a taxonomic suggestion until ruled on by the International Commission on Zoological Nomenclature, but the body has so far not supported the change and has not addressed the taxonomic suggestion, thus the official taxonomy remains *Elaphe*.

Researchers rejected the taxonomic change to *Pantherophis*, preferring to retain the current concept of *Elaphe* and the spelling *obsoleta*.

Rat Snakes in Captivity

Rat snakes are commonly kept as pets by reptile enthusiasts. The corn snake is one of the most popular pet reptiles, and belongs to the rat snake family. New world species are generally thought to be more docile in captivity as opposed to old world rat snakes, of which the opposite is assumed.

16 Kingsnakes and Milksnakes

Kingsnakes and milksnakes are members of one of the most popular snake genera in herpetoculture, *Lampropeltis*. The genus *Lampropeltis* is endemic to North and South America, with many members present in the continental United States.

The most popular kingsnakes in the reptile keeping hobby include the California kingsnake (*Lampropeltis getula califoniae*), and grey-banded kingsnake (*Lampropeltis alterna*), among others. The most popular milksnakes include the pueblan (*L.t. campbelli*), the sinaloan (*L.t. sinaloae*), and the honduran (*L.t. hondurensis*).

Members of this genus are rightfully popular with reptile keepers, they are hardy, easy to breed, and come in a dazzling array of beautiful colour and pattern morphs. This care sheet is intended to cover the basic care of both kingsnakes and milksnakes for beginning reptile enthusiasts. We also highly encourage new hobbyists to purchase captive care books to help them keep and breed this genus successfully.

Kingsnakes and milksnakes come in a variety of sizes, so a cage can be chosen according to the adult size of the snake, although smaller cages can obviously be used when the animal is growing, in fact, smaller cages for young snakes can be better in some instances because it is easier for the snake to find the food. All baby kingsnakes and milksnakes can be housed in an enclosure the size of a standard ten gallon aquarium, or even the size of a five gallon aquarium, depending on how often one wishes to purchase a larger enclosure as the animal grows.

Most adult kingsnakes can be housed in a standard twenty-gallon long or thirty-gallon breeder aquarium. The idea is to have an enclosure large enough to provide a thermal gradient. Many hobbyist and professional breeders do not utilize glass aquariums because of their bulk and weight.

If you are planning on owning more than ten or so snakes, it may be advisable to purchase a rack system or stackable reptile enclosures. A rack system looks similar to a chest of drawers, there are several rows of cages, one on top of the other, all encased in one larger cabinet-like piece. In each row there are either one, or several (depending on the size of the individual cages) plastic cages. These cages pull out from the cabinet like a drawer does from a chest.

Many rack systems are 'lidless'; they are built so that the cages slide back in flush with the bottom of the next row, which acts like a lid. Running along the back of the rack system is a line of heat tape which heats one end of the enclosure, providing a thermal gradient. Heat tape must be controlled by a thermostat in order to provide the ideal "hot spot" temperature and to avoid a fire hazard. Rack systems allow herpetoculturists to keep snakes more efficiently and to provide the correct thermal gradient.

Other options for reptile housing include manufactured cages, there are many companies specializing in custom reptile enclosures, if you are interested in these, ask us for a reference.

There are a variety of different choices to use for covering the bottom of the enclosure. Cedar and pine shavings (as used with small mammals) should be avoided as the aromatic oils from these products irritate the respiratory system of snakes and they tend to get little pieces of the stuff stuck in their mouths when they eat. Sterilized reptile bark is one choice, it is attractive and easy to clean, just lift out the poop when needed, and replace all the substrate once a month Aspen bedding can also be used, it has the benefits of bark and allows snakes to burrow, creating their own hiding spots. Less aesthetic but certainly functional choices include paper towels, newspaper, Astroturf, and cut-to-fit liners.

It is important to provide snakes with hiding areas so that they feel secure in their captive environment. Hiding areas can be made out of old margarine tubs turned upside down with a hole cut in the side, cardboard shoeboxes, or my personal favorite, terracotta plant saucers with access holes knocked in the side (these come in many different sizes, are cheap, and easy to find at any greenhouse or home supply store).

Many reptile product retailers also carry plastic premade hiding spots, which may be a little more expensive, but are durable and easy to clean. Several hiding spots, at least two, one on the warm side and one on the cool side, should be included in any snake enclosure.

The most important factor for keeping kingsnakes and milksnakes (all reptiles actually) is providing the correct environmental conditions. Caring for reptiles is very different than caring for other pets because reptiles are what are called ectothermic. Ectothermic, which is sometimes called 'cold-blooded', means that reptiles do not maintain a stable body temperature by creating heat from their metabolism.

Reptiles rely on a behavioural mechanism called thermoregulation to regulate their body temperature. What this means is that when a reptile is too hot, it moves into the shade or down into its den to cool down, and when it needs to heat up (to digest food for example) it basks in the sun or moves into a warmer area.

This is important for reptile keepers to understand because in captivity, we determine what temperatures a reptile has access to. Reptile keepers must provide a thermal gradient for their animals so that they may heat up or cool down, as they would do in the wild.

There are many different ways to provide a themal gradient, but all require that you purchase a good digital thermometer to make sure you are providing the correct temperature range.

Almost all kingsnakes and milksnakes do well with a maintenance temperature gradient of 84-88° F on the warm end and 70-75° at the cool end. At night, the temperature can safely drop to 65° F as long as the snake can warm up during the day. If you are using an aquarium to house your snake, one good choice is to purchase an undertank heater. Undertank heaters are made out of flexible plastic and work a lot like a regular heating pad.

One side of the heater is adhesive and this side attached to the bottom of the outside of the aquarium. It is important to place the heater on one end of the cage, so that the other end remains cooler. Undertank heaters work well because they can be left on a night without disturbing the animal. The other choice is a heat bulb. The heat bulb must be located on one end of the enclosure and most not be accessible to the snake (to prevent burns). One method that works well is to have a screen top with a clamp light sitting on top of one end of the cage.

The wattage of the bulb necessary to provide the correct temperature will vary with the ambient temperature, so it is best to test the heat light by leaving it on for a few hours and monitoring the temperature closely. If the heat area provided is too hot, the snake will still use it because it must warm up to digest it's food properly, but it can be seriously injured by thermal burns in the process, which brings me to the subject of heat rocks.

We do not use nor recommend heat rocks for any reptile at all. The reason why is that heat rocks provide a small, localized heat source which is fully accessible to the reptile. Heat rocks often have 'hot spots' and can overheat quickly, possibly causing severe thermal burns. If a reptile is housed in an enclosure that is cold everywhere except a tiny little heat rock, it will spend most of it's time curled around, and in direct contact with, this unstable heat source, even to the point of causing severe injury to itself. Our advice is to find other, safer, heating alternatives.

Another aspect of providing the correct environmental conditions is humidity. Most kingsnakes and milksnakes do well with the relative humidity ranging from 40-60 per cent.

Relative humidity becomes and important issue before a snake is about to shed. Snakes shed at variable intervals, with more sheds as a snake is growing. When a snake is close to shedding its skin, its eyes will become milky and its scales will become duller.

Then this will clear up and a few days after that, the snake will shed. When you notice your snake beginning to shed, the humidity must be increased to aid in this processes. Most incomplete sheds are caused by low humidity. One way to raise the humidity is to mist the cage lightly for a few days until the snake sheds. Also, a humidity box can be put in, and left in the enclosure for the snake to use whenever it needs to.

Humidity boxes can be easily and cheaply constructed out of plastic Rubbermaid containers large enough to house a loosely coiled snake. An access hole must be cut in the side, but otherwise the box should remain closed. A layer of moist moss such as sphagnum or peat should be put inside the humidity box and kept moist at all times. Moist paper towels work as well and are easier to replace but tend to try out more quickly. With baby snakes, a deli cup can be used to make a humidity box.

All snakes are carnivores; they eat only other animals. Baby king and milksnakes do best on a diet of pinky mice, generally one or two pinky mice once a week. As the snake grows, so should its prey. A general rule of thumb is to feed a snake a food item that is as large, or slightly larger, than the diameter of the snake at its widest point (excluding the head).

King and milksnakes, specifically the California kingsnake, will often eat other snakes of the same size if given the opportunity, so it is best to house each snake individually to avoid this problem. In fact, rattlesnakes make up a significant part of the diet of wild California kingsnakes! When purchasing a new snake, it is very important to purchase only baby snakes that have eaten unaltered domestic pinky mice at least once but preferably more. Reputable breeders do not sell baby snakes that have not eaten (unless they tell you so) and will often provide you with a record of the baby snake's feedings (at herp shows this is often written on the bottom of the for sale container).

This is especially important with the 'problem feeding' species such as the grey-banded kingsnake, whose babies are notoriously difficult to get feeding on pinky mice. Make sure you check this before you buy!!

In our opinion, it is best to feed freshly killed or frozen prey that has been thawed.

The reason for this recommendation is that dead mice don't bite! If a live mouse is left in a cage with a snake that is not hungry, it can cause significant harm to the snake by chewing on it. If you must feed live, make sure to watch and make sure the snake eats, don't drop the prey in and leave.

Most pet stores carry feeder mice, but if you have more than a few snakes, it is much more economical to either raise your own rodents or buy them mail order.

There are many people who raise feeder rodents and advertise in the classifieds section of the major reptile trade magazines.

Occasionally, a snake may refuse to feed. Food refusal is caused by a number of things such as incorrect environmental conditions, a shed phase, pregnancy, or illness. If you snake refuses food for more than four weeks, has the correct environmental conditions (including hiding spots), is not shedding and has never been with a member of the opposite sex, it should be checked for illness.

Some snakes will refuse food in the wintertime, even if provided with the correct environmental conditions and if they are not sick, shedding, or gravid. These snakes are acting upon their instinct to hibernate and should be allowed to do so. Most *Lampropeltis* hibernate for some time during the cool season. To hibernate your kingsnake or milksnake, make sure it has no food for two weeks but still has access to a warm spot so that it can remove all material from its digestive tract.

After this time, the temperature should be lowered gradually to between 60-65°. The snake should not be fed during this time, but fresh drinking water should be provided. Leave the snake in these conditions, checking on it frequently for signs of illness, for 4-6 weeks. After this time, slowly warm the animal back up to its maintenance temperature and offer food. Hibernation is often helpful if one wishes to breed their snakes.

Regurgitation is a common problem with captive king and milksnakes. Regurgitation can be caused by handling a snake soon after it has eaten (don't), too cool temperatures, illness, or feeding a prey item that is too large.

If your snake barfs more than twice, and has the correct environmental conditions and has been fed appropriately sized food, take it to a herp vet.

17 Indian Cobra

Naja naja or the Indian cobra is a species of venomous snake found in the Indian subcontinent. It is one of the 'big four', four snake species that are responsible for causing the most snakebites in India. This snake is revered in Indian mythology and culture, and is often seen with snake charmers. It is now protected in India under the Indian Wildlife Protection Act (1972).

On the rear of the snake's hood are two circular ocelli patterns connected by a curved line, evoking the image of spectacles. It is believed by Hindus that those are the feet markings of Krishna who danced on Kaliya snake's head. An average cobra is about 1.9 meters (6 feet) in length and rarely as long as 2.4 meters (nearly 8 feet). The spectacle pattern on the hood is varies greatly, as does the overall colour of the snake.

The Oriental Ratsnake *Ptyas mucosus* is often mistaken for the cobra; however this snake is much longer and can easily be distinguished by the more prominent ridged appearance of its body. Other snakes that resemble *Naja naja* are the Banded Racer *Argyrogena fasciolata* and the Indian Smooth Snake *Coronella brachyura*.

The genus name *Naja* comes from Indian Languages. The Indian Cobra or Spectacled Cobra, being common in South Asia, is referred to by a number of local names deriving from the root of *Naag* (Hindi, Sanskrit, Oriya, Marathi), *Moorkan* (Malayalam), *Naya* (Singhalese), *Naaga Pamu* (Telugu), *Nagara*

Haavu (Kannada), *Nalla pambu* or *Naja Pambu* (Tamil) and *Gokhra* (Bengali). The most distinctive and impressive characteristic of the Indian cobra is the hood, which it forms by raising the anterior portion of the body and spreading some of the ribs in its neck region when it is threatened.

The Indian cobra is native to the Indian subcontinent which includes present day Pakistan, India, Bangladesh and Sri Lanka. It can be found in plains, jungles, open fields and the regions heavily populated by people. Its distribution ranges from sea-level up to 2000m. Cobras normally feed on rodents, toads, frogs, birds and snakes. Its diet of rats leads it to areas inhabited by humans including farms and outskirts of urban areas. Indian cobras are oviparous and lay their eggs between the months of April and July. The female snake usually lays from 10 to 30 eggs in rat holes or termite mounds and the eggs hatch 48 to 69 days later. Newborn cobras measure between 8 and 12 inches (20-30 cm). The young when hatched are exact replicas of the parents and have fully functional venom glands.

The Indian cobra's venom contains a powerful post-synaptic neurotoxin. The venom acts on the synaptic gaps of the nerves, thereby paralyzing muscles, and in severe bites leading to respiratory failure or cardiac arrest. The venom components include enzymes such as hyaluronidase that cause lysis and increase the spread of the venom. The toxicity of its venom is similar to that of the Chinese cobra and it is one of the most venomous *Naja* species based on LD_{50} value in mice. Symptoms of cobra envenomation can begin from 15 minutes to two hours after the bite, and can be fatal in less than an hour.

The Indian Cobra is one of the Big four and a polyvalent serum is available for treating snakebites by these snakes. Zedoary, a local spice with a reputation for being effective against snakebite, has shown promise in experiments testing its activity against cobra venom.

The venom of young cobras has been used as a substance of abuse in India, with cases of snake charmers being paid for providing bites from their snakes. Symptoms included loss of consciousness, euphoria, and sedation. Though this practice is outdated now.

The spectacled cobra is much respected and feared, and even has its own place in Hindu mythology as a powerful deity. The Hindu god Shiva is often depicted with a protective cobra coiled around his neck. Vishnu, the preserver of the universe, is usually portrayed as reclining on the coiled body of Sheshnag, the *Preeminent Serpent*, a giant snake deity with multiple cobra heads. Cobras are also worshipped during the Hindu festival of *Nag Panchami*.

There are numerous myths about cobras in India, including the idea that they mate with ratsnakes.

Snake Charming

The Indian cobra's celebrity comes from its popularity as a snake of choice for snake charmers. The cobra's dramatic threat posture makes for a unique spectacle as it appears to sway to the tune of a snake charmer's flute. Snake charmers with their cobras in a wicker basket are a common sight in many parts of India only during the Nag Panchami festival. The cobra is deaf to the snake charmer's pipe, but follows the visual cue of the moving pipe and it can sense the ground vibrations from the snake charmer's tapping. In the past Indian snake charmers also conducted cobra and mongoose fights. These gory fight shows, in which the snake was usually killed, are now illegal.

There are different types of cobras as the Indian Cobra, Monocellate Cobra, King Cobra etc. Local Names: Bengali: *Naga* (*gokurra binocellate* form), *Keauthia* (monocellate form); *Pushtu Chajitiwalla*; Tamil: *Nalla pambu, Naga pambu*; Kannada: *Nagara havu*; Malayalam: *Moorkan, Surpam; Singhalese Naya*. The species name of the Indian Cobra is *naja*. It is a harmful snake and has a small 'cuneate' scale between the 4th and 5th infralabials and there is a preocular touching the intranasal, and also there is the presence of a 3rd supralabial in contact with the eye. The elongated ribs of the 3rd and 27th vertebrae form the hood of the snake. The 9th rib on the left and 10th rib on the right are the longest, the preceding and succeeding ribs are shortened. The head of the cobras are depressed with a short and round snout. Its nostrils are large and pupils are round. There is a swelling at the temporal region over the underlying poison glands. There are distinct grooves on its spine. The cobras are variable in coloration and markings. Three races of cobras are recognized on the basis of the hood pattern. One is the 'spectacled' or binocellatc cobra of peninsular India (*Naja naja naja*), which is yellowish, brownish or black above with or without a black and white mark on hood, a black and white spoon the inside of the hood with one or two black crossbars below hood. The second variety is the Sri Lankan and south Indian cobras that are brown in color and have well defined hood marks. Cobras from the north are black and the hood is absent in some of them.

Monocellate Cobra (*Naja naja kaouthia*) differs from the other cobras in having a single yellow or orange O-shaped mark on the hood. They are olive brown or black in color. This is the common Cobra found in eastern India and eastwards of India. The Black Cobra (*Naja naja oxiana*) occurs in the extreme northwest. In the younger stages they are light grey or brown and have dark crossbars. Adults are brown or black. The cobras are eclectic in habitat. They are found almost anywhere, in heavy jungle, open cultivated land, populated areas etc. They are often found near or in water. It is often timid but aggressive when disturbed. The young ones are more dangerous than the adults. They are more easily excited and are ready to strike repeatedly and with determination. When exited the cobras raise their fore body and sway backwards and forward hissing The throat becomes pouched and the whole body is inflated. It flickers its tongue in and out during inhalation and exhalation. When the snake bites its prey, and if the poison is not injected the first time, the poison is ejected as a spray. The cobra feeds on rats, frogs, toads, birds, lizards and other snakes including other cobras. It also eats eggs. Eggs are swallowed as a whole and digested in about 48 hours. Its mating season is in January and majority of eggs are laid in April/May. The period of gestation is about sixty-two days but may extend considerably. Eggs hatch in 48 to 69 days. 45 eggs are deposited at a time. The eggs are soft-shelled elongate and oval measuring 49 × 28 mm. The parents live together before pairing and one or both guard the eggs. Both parents known to keep warm the eggs. The poison glands are active from birth.

There are two fully operative canaliculate fangs on each side. These are shed singly at intervals. The fangs are about seven mm in length. The poison glands are similar to the parotid salivary glands in mammals and have the shape and size of an almond kernel. The venom is a clear, viscid fluid resembling olive oil in appearance. The amount of venom secreted varies with age, vitality and temper of the animal. The poison acts mainly as a neurotoxin and blood and cell destroyer. The neurotoxin paralyses the respiratory center and is the chief cause of death. Other deadly effects of the venom are loss of clotting power of the blood and destruction of red blood cells. The symptoms are a stinging or burning plan accompanied by swelling and oozing of bloodstained serum. The effects are gradual but rapidly advancing paralysis commences with the legs, the neck droops, the muscles of the tongue, lips, and throat, are affected and speech becomes difficult. The lower lip falls and allows saliva to dribble, swallowing becomes difficult or impossible. Breathing becomes difficult, laborious and stops. Other symptoms are vomiting and hemorrhage from the various orifices of the body.

The bite of a cobra is not fatal at all times. Fatality depends on the quantity of venom injected, the natural resistance of the victim, the condition of the snake and various other factors. The Haffkine Institute's polyvalent serum is fully effective even when symptoms are far advanced.

King Cobra (*Ophiophagus hannah*) Local Names: Oriya: *Ahi raj*; Bengali: *Sankha chur, Sha-khamuti; Assai Fetty sap; Shan Oni son-an; Karen Oni thaw*; Tamil: *Krishna nar Karunagam*; Malayalam: *Krishna sarpam, Karinchathii*; Kannada: *Kaj havu, Nagin, Kalinagin.*

The species name of the King Cobra is *hannah*. The King Cobra is also known as *Hamadryad*. It is the third largest snake in India. Its body is robust and the scales are glossy. The 'hood' is dilatable than in the cobra. Its head is flat and snout is round. Its pupil is round. It has occipital shields on its body. The adults are blackish brown or light brown and have a round tail. Bands become obscure with age and they become more evident under excitement. The color of the head is olivaceous-brown. Its throat is creamy to dull orange in color. The hatchlings are intense black with pure white bands. It is a highly dangerous snake. King Cobras like the other snakes smell using their forked tongues, which has the capacity to pick up scented particles and transfer them to a special sensory receptor located at the roof of the mouth. When it scents the smell of a meal or a prey, it will flick its tongue to detect the prey's direction. It has an excellent eyes sight, outstanding intelligence and sensitivity to vibrations compared to other cobra species. It swallows the prey as a whole and its toxins begin the digestion of the victim. It does not have rigidly fixed jaws but has extremely pliable ligaments, enabling the lower jawbones to move independently of each other. After a large meal the snake may live for many months without another meal due to a very slow metabolic rate. King Cobras are able to hunt at all times of day, although it is rarely seen at night, leading some to erroneously classify it as a diurnal species.

18 Spitting Cobra

A spitting cobra is one of several species of cobras that have the ability to eject venom from their fangs when defending themselves against predators. The sprayed venom is harmless to intact skin. However, it can cause permanent blindness if introduced to the eye and left untreated (causing chemosis and corneal swelling).

Despite their name, these snakes do not actually spit their venom. The venom sprays out in distinctive geometric patterns, using muscular contractions upon the venom glands. These muscles squeeze the glands and force the venom out through forward-facing holes at the tips of the fangs. The explanation that a large gust of air is expelled from the lung to propel the venom forward has been proven wrong. When cornered, some species can 'spit' their venom a distance as great as 2 meters (6.6 ft). While spitting is typically their primary form of defense, all spitting cobras are capable of delivering venom through a bite as well. Most species' venom exhibit significant hemotoxic effects, along with more typical neurotoxic effects of other cobra species.

SPECIES OF THE SPITTING COBRAS

African

- *Naja ashei*
- *Naja katiensis*
- *Naja mossambica*
- *Naja nigricollis*
- *Naja nigricincta*

- *Naja nubiae*
- *Naja pallida*

Asiatic

- *Naja philippinensis*
- *Naja samarensis*
- *Naja siamensis*
- *Naja sputatrix*
- *Naja sumatrana*

Other Spitting Species

Some non-spitting cobras and vipers have been noted to spit occasionally. Certain predominantly non-spitting Asian cobras have the spitting tendency. The Rinkhals cobra (*Hemachatus haemachatus*) is another elapid species, which, while not belonging to the Cobra genus *Naja*, is closely related and is capable of spitting venom.

It has been reported that several viper species (notably the Mangshan Pitviper) may 'fling' or even spit venom forward in a spray when threatened. These sprays are often very consistent.

Red Spitting Cobra

The Red Spitting Cobra (*Naja pallida*), is a species of spitting cobra native to Africa. This species is one of several spittings cobra in Africa. Spitting cobras do not spit their venom. Instead, they *spray* their venom to their enemies, and if the venom gets into the eyes, it can cause intense pain and temporary or even permanent blindness.

This is a relatively small-sized cobra, with maximum length of 120 cm (4 ft) and smaller sized specimen of about 60 cm (2 ft) to 75 cm (2 ft 6 in). Body colour of this species has great variation from red, deep orange, pale red, pinkish and light brown. Red Spitting Cobras found in Northern Africa have duller colour while others are much brighter. There is a black band on the underside of the neck. Like most other spitting cobras, the hood of the Red Spitting Cobra is narrow compared with the Indian Cobra and the Cape Cobra. It also has a small round head and a pair of rather large eyes.

Distribution and Habitat

The Red Spitting Cobra is mainly found in Eastern Africa, including Kenya and Sudan. It primarily inhabits dry savanna and semi-desert area. It is quite common to be found in oasis in desert where it hunts.

Behaviour

Adults are more commonly found at night while juveniles are active both during day and night. This is a terrestrial, fast and alert snake. When threatened, it rears up and displays a typical cobra hood. It also hisses loudly. If the intruder does not retreat, it may sprays jets of venom to the face of the intruder. Venom that gets into the eyes can cause burning pain and blindness. Even so, this snake seldom bites and causes human death, as this species rarely encounter people due to its habitat and this species is not aggressive.

This species has a wide range of prey, including small mammals, lizards, other snakes, birds and eggs.

Venom

This species, like most spitting cobra, contains a mixture of neurotoxic and cytotoxic. Bite symptoms include slight pain around the wound and numbness of lips and tongue. Although it rarely causes human death, urgent medical care is required if someone is bitten by this species.

Reproduction

The Red Spitting Cobra is oviparous. The female will lay around 5 to 15 eggs.

Taxonomy

This species was formerly considered to be a subspecies, *Naja mossambica pallida*, of *Naja mossambica*, but is now categorized as a separate species. Indeed *mossambica* is more closely related to *N. nigricollis* than to this species. The Red Spitting Cobra is closely related and forms a sister taxon with the Nubian Spitting Cobra (*Naja nubiae*) of northern Africa, which was originally considered a northern population of *pallida* before being recognized as a distinct species in 2003.

The Spitting Cobra is most renowned for their infamously remarkable *spitting fangs* that allow the cobra to actually spray venom accurately into the face and eyes of predators and trampling hoovestock. When the cobra wants to 'Spit' or 'Spray' its venom at a threat, it 'Hoods Up', aims its open mouth as specialized muscles contract the Venom Gland, forcing the Cobra's Venom out through its fangs. Spitting Cobra are extremely accurate at distances over 10 feet. Some scientists theorize that the 'Spitting Behaviour' and evolution of the fang modifications were a result of the fact that Spitting cobras cohabitate with numerous antelope species. These scientists believe that thc primary function of Spitting cobra fangs is to deter being trampled by antelope hooves. The Cobra is well equipped to spray its painful venom directly into the eyes of potential trampling animals from a safe distance. This theory is almost identical to the theory of the cvolution of the 'Rattlesnake Rattle' on rattlesnakes. Scientists speculate that the rattle's main function was to alert buffalo and other grazing North American Hoovestock to their presence in order to avoid being trampled by their feet.

Spitting Cobras prefer to spit or spray venom into the eyes of would be attackers, threats or predators, but are perfectly capable of delivering a deadly Snake envenomation via a bite. In fact, Spitting Cobra Bites are common in some areas of Africa and are extremely painful if not deadly. In many cases, victims of Spitting Cobra Attacks become permanently blind if sprayed in the eyes. Spitting Cobra venom is very toxic and extremely deadly, although it is nothing compared to the venom of the King Cobra, which also delivers a lot of venom with each hit. But then again, being shot by a 9 mm vs. a 45 still sucks big time, if you get my drift. So in reality, Spitting Cobra poison is the lesser of the two evils compared to King Cobra Poison.

Spitting Cobras in Captivity are much easier to care for than the King Cobra as they do not feed exclusively on snakes. Instead, Spitting Cobras feed primarily on small rodents, frogs, toads and even lizards. Captive breeding is achieved on a common basis with some specimens living over 20 years. Spitting Cobra eggs are laid under logs, in abandoned rodent burrows, termite nests or other suitable nooks and crannies. Baby Spitting Cobras are born "Locked and Loaded" and pack a mean wallop if bitten. An interesting fact about captive Spitting Cobras is that the majority of them loose their desire or need to "Spray" their venom. Not that they won't bite the be-geezers out of you if given the opportunity, they will. Most cobras are very intelligent and hate wasting venom if not necessary. Perhaps captive Cobras being fed a commercial diet of thawed rodents realize their caretaker will not 'Step' on them? Who knows for sure, but many Spitting Cobras seem to lose there spitting urges in captivity. Then again, there are those individual specimens that are constantly spraying venom at any passerby. These are a major pain to manage in captivity, as you always have to wipe down their enclosure.

19 Cape Cobra

The Cape Cobra (*Naja nivea*) is a moderately sized cobra inhabiting the arid regions of Southern Africa. It averages four feet (120 cm) long but may grow to be six feet (180 cm) long. The colour varies from location to location, and those from the Kalahari are normally bright uniform yellow or yellow with brown speckles uniformly all over the body.

Behaviour

This snake is diurnal: it is primarily active during the day and early evening. It feeds on a wide spectrum of prey, including other snakes, and tends to climb low trees and raid weaver bird colonies. It is also attracted to rodents. Cape Cobras are great climbers.

Venom

The cape cobra produces a powerful neurotoxin that affects the respiratory system. Without proper antivenom treatment the mortality rate in humans is 60 per cent and death normally occurs 2-5 hours after being bitten and is usually as a result of respiratory failure because of the onset of paralysis. The snake is quick to strike and becomes aggressive if cornered, but given its native environment, it is likely to retreat. Its main predators are various species of raptors inhabiting the area and mainly the mongoose, along with honey badger or ratel.

Reproduction

The Cape Cobra is also known as the 'geelslang' (yellow snake) and 'bruinkapel' (brown cobra). Afrikaans speaking

South Africans refer to the Cape Cobra as 'koperkapel', mainly because of a rich yellow colour variation. It has the most potent venom of all African cobras.

The Cape cobra, *Naja nivea,* is a commonmonotypic elapid species in the Western Cape, and is responsible for most fatal incidents of snakebite in the province.

The venom is also the most potent of all the South African cobras. It is perhaps therefore surprising that virtually nothing is known about the ecology, habitats and behaviour of this widespread and potentially dangerous species.

Naja nivea is a habitat generalist, and can be found in a wide variety of biomes across southwestern Africa, including dune thicket, coastal and mountain fynbos, karroid sandveld, and semi desert. Unlike most other African cobras this species shows a wide range of colour variation; from yellow and golden brown to dark brown and black. In addition, individuals show a varying degree of black or pale stippling and blotches, and although it has been stated that colour and marking are geographically related, it is also possible to observe virtually all colour varieties at one location.

For example, it is well known that the Kalahari specimens in Botswana are usually more consistently yellow than the more southerly populations. However, at DeHoop, and other specific locations in the Western Cape, all colour variations have been recorded. It is not a particularly large cobra; average adult size is around 1.5 metres, and females are somewhat smaller than males. The largest specimen recorded at DeHoop was a male with a total length of 1.85 metres.

The Cape cobra is a timid snake, always seeking to escape when encountered, although when aroused it has been described as willing to bite readily. It has also been stated that the Cape cobra is more aggressive during the mating period.

However, passive observation of another notorious South African elapid, the Black mamba, *Dendroaspis polylepis,* has shown that in normal circumstances this species exhibits alert but calm behaviour. Observations of the Cape cobra at refugia so far at DeHoop have indicated very similar behaviour. The Cape cobra is a diurnal species and actively forages throughout the day.

During very hot weather it may become crepuscular, but is rarely if ever observed during the hours of darkness. There is no current information with regard to size of home range, population densities, or sex ratio. Detailed accounts of such as reproductive and feeding behaviour are also lacking, and past and current information has tended to be anecdotal, or repetitive in popular literature. For example, the accounts of the Cape cobra climbing and preying on sociable weaver (*Philetaurus socius*) in the Kalahari has been quoted many times.

Researchers states that the Cape cobra uses rodent burrows and other animal holes as a more or less permanent retreat, but other information regarding sedentary behaviour or the occupation of permanent refugia also appear to be anecdotal.

20 Cobra Venom

Among snakes, cobras and coral snakes may be singled out as having a particularly neurotoxic venom; among other animals, the venom of arachnids also falls into the neurotoxic category. The spitting cobra can spray its venom from a distance of about 2.4 m (about 8 ft) into the eyes of its victims, causing temporary blindness and great pain. Venom coming in contact with human eyes causes an immediate and severe irritation of the conjunctiva and cornea that, if untreated, may result in permanent blindness. The venom of cobras, a neurotoxin, acts powerfully on the nervous system. With effective serum more available, however, the high death rate from cobra bites in some areas of Asia has decreased. Cobra venom has been used for many years in medical research because it has an enzyme, lecithinase, that dissolves cell walls as well as membranes surrounding viruses.

A common misconception is that baby snake are deadlier than adults. While not proven scientifically, it would seem that an adult cobra can control the the amount of venom delivered, if any, with each bite, depending on the threat it feels. A baby snake has no control over the amount of venom delivered by its bite, thus always giving a full dose. A baby cobra is fully able to defend itself in as little as three hours after entering the world. Cobras are completely immune to the venom produced by their species.

Venom

Poison of animal origin, usually restricted to poisons that are administered by biting or stinging and used to capture—

and, sometimes, aid in digesting—prey, or for defense. Thus the poisons secreted by the skin of some toads, or accumulated in the bodies of numerous inedible animals, are ordinarily not considered venoms. The most familiar venomous animals are certain snakes and insects and the spiders and other arachnids.

Venomous species occur throughout the animal kingdom, however, including the mammals. Some shrews, for example, have venomous saliva, and the platypus bears poison spurs on its hind legs. The severity of a venom's effects depends on several factors, such as its chemical nature, the stinging or biting mechanism involved, the amount of venom delivered, and the size and condition of the victim. For example, all spiders are venomous, but the venoms of most are too weak or minute in quantity to have noticeable effects on humans; in addition, many spiders cannot even puncture human skin. Thus, few of them are poisonous to humans, but their venoms are quite effective on insect prey.

Chemically, venoms vary greatly across the animal kingdom and are not readily defined. Snake venoms, for example, are complex mixtures of enzymatic proteins and different toxins. In terms of their effects, however, they may be broadly categorized as hemotoxic (damaging blood vessels and causing hemorrhage) or neurotoxic (paralyzing nerve centers that control respiration and heart action); they may also contain agents that promote or prevent blood clotting. Sometimes a combination of these effects is involved, however, and variations may occur within genera or even within species.

The effects of insect stings are usually the result of histamines that produce local irritation and swelling. Serums against various venoms can be produced by injecting animals such as horses with sublethal doses and extracting the immune serum, or antivenin, that the animal body produces. Venoms themselves have occasional medicinal uses; for example, some are used as painkillers in cases of arthritis or cancer, and some serve as coagulants for people with hemophilia.

Note the distinction between *venomous* and *poisonous*: *venomous* refers to a creature that has the ability to secrete or utilize it's venom externally, while *poisonous* includes creatures that contain a poison substance. Often poisonous creatures are harmless unless eaten. Venomous creatures can often use their poison as a weapon. Cobras are all venomous, yet most are not poisonous, so long as the venom glands are not eaten.

Venom Strength Comparison

- Quantity venom delivered
- Lethal human dose

NAME OF SNAKE

Various Cobras

- 150-350 mg
- 18-45 mg

Various Sea Snakes

- 1-15 mg
- 2-4mg

Indian Krait

- 8-20 mg
- 3 mg

Eastern Corel Snake

- 3-5 mg
- 4 mg

Tiger Snake

- 35-65 mg
- 3 mg

Australian Brown Snake

- 5-10 mg
- 3 mg

Mambas

- 6-100 mg
- 12-15 mg

Puff Adder

- 160-200 mg
- 95 mg

Gaboon Viper

- 450-600 mg
- 180 mg

American Copperhead

- 40-70 mg
- 100 mg

Cottonmouth Moccasin

- 100-150 mg
- 125 mg

Rattle Snakes

Eastern Diamond Black

- 400-700 mg
- 100 mg

Western Diamond Black

- 200-300 mg
- 100 mg

Timber

- 100-150 mg
- 75 mg

Mojave

- 50-90 mg
- 15 mg

Bushmaster

- 200-400 mg
- 150 mg

References

Behler, John L.; King, F. Wayne (1979). *The Audubon Society Field Guide to Reptiles and Amphibians of North America*. New York: Alfred A. Knopf. p. 581. ISBN 0394508246.

Bullfinch, Thomas (2000). *Bullfinch's Complete Mythology*. London: Chancellor Press. p. 679. ISBN 0753703815.

Capula, Massimo; Behler (1989). *Simon & Schuster's Guide to Reptiles and Amphibians of the World*. New York: Simon & Schuster. ISBN 0671690981.

Coborn, John (1991). *The Atlas of Snakes of the World*. New Jersey: TFH Publications. ISBN 9780866227490.

Cogger, Harold; Zweifel, Richard (1992). *Reptiles & Amphibians*. Sydney: Weldon Owen. ISBN 0831727861.

Conant, Roger; Collins, Joseph (1991). *A Field Guide to Reptiles and Amphibians Eastern/Central North America*. Boston, Massachusetts: Houghton Mifflin Company. ISBN 0395583896.

Deane, John (1833). *The Worship of the Serpent*. Whitefish, Montana: Kessinger Publishing. p. 412. ISBN 1564598985.

Ditmars, Raymond L (1906). *Poisonous Snakes of the United States: How to Distinguish Them*. New York: E.R. Sanborn. p. 11.

Ditmars, Raymond L (1931). *Snakes of the World*. New York: Macmillan. p. 11. ISBN 978-0025317307.

Ditmars, Raymond L (1933). *Reptiles of the World: The Crocodilians, Lizards, Snakes, Turtles and Tortoises of the Eastern and Western Hemispheres*. New York: Macmillan. p. 321.

Ditmars, Raymond L; W. Bridges (1935). *Snake-Hunters' Holiday*. New York: D. Appleton and Company. p. 309.

Ditmars, Raymond L (1939). *A Field Book of North American Snakes*. Garden City, New York: Doubleday, Doran & Co. p. 305.

Freiberg, Dr. Marcos; Walls, Jerry (1984). *The World of Venomous Animals*. New Jersey: TFH Publications. ISBN 0876665679.

Gibbons, J. Whitfield; Gibbons, Whit (1983). *Their Blood Runs Cold: Adventures With Reptiles and Amphibians*. Alabama: University of Alabama Press. p. 164. ISBN 978-0817301354.

Mattison, Chris (2007). *The New Encyclopedia of Snakes*. New Jersey: Princeton University Press. p. 272. ISBN 978-0691132952.

McDiarmid, RW; Campbell, JA; Touré, T (1999). *Snake Species of the World: A Taxonomic and Geographic Reference*. 1. Herpetologists' League. p. 511. ISBN 1893777006.

Mehrtens, John (1987). *Living Snakes of the World in Colour*. New York: Sterling. ISBN 0806964618.

Nóbrega Alves, RôMulo Romeu; Silva Vieira, Washington Luiz; Santana, Gindomar Gomes (2008). "Reptiles Used in Traditional Folk Medicine: Conservation Implications". *Biodiversity and Conservation* 17 (8): 2037-2049.

Romulus Whitaker (English edition); Tamil translation by O.Henry Francis (1996). *(Snakes around us, Tamil)*. National Book Trust. ISBN 81-237-1905-1.

Rosenfeld, Arthur (1989). *Exotic Pets*. New York: Simon & Schuster. p. 293. ISBN 067147654.

Spawls, Steven; Branch, Bill (1995). *The Dangerous Snakes of Africa*. Sanibel Island, Florida: Ralph Curtis Publishing. p. 192. ISBN 0883590298.

Index